an alphabetic bitmap narrative of the endless society

Logokons

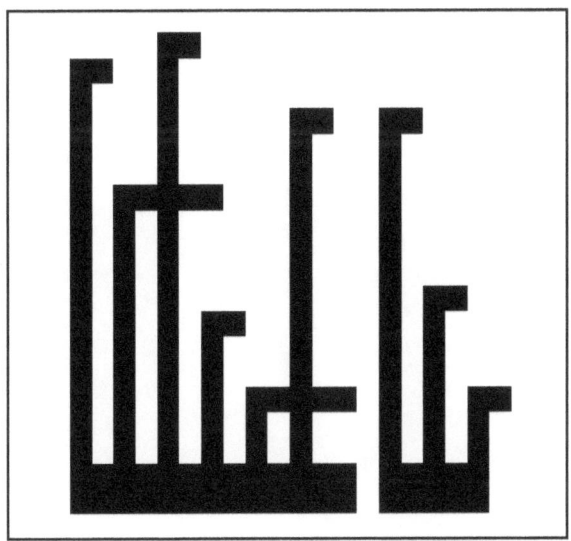

by mIEKAL aND & Liaizon Wakest

1992/2006
Xerox Sutra Editions
dreamtime village, wisconsin

ISBN 1-4404-3437-9
978-1-4404-3437-2

Xerox Sutra Editions
10375 Cty Hway Alphabet
La Farge, WI 54639

for Lyx

these will always be for you

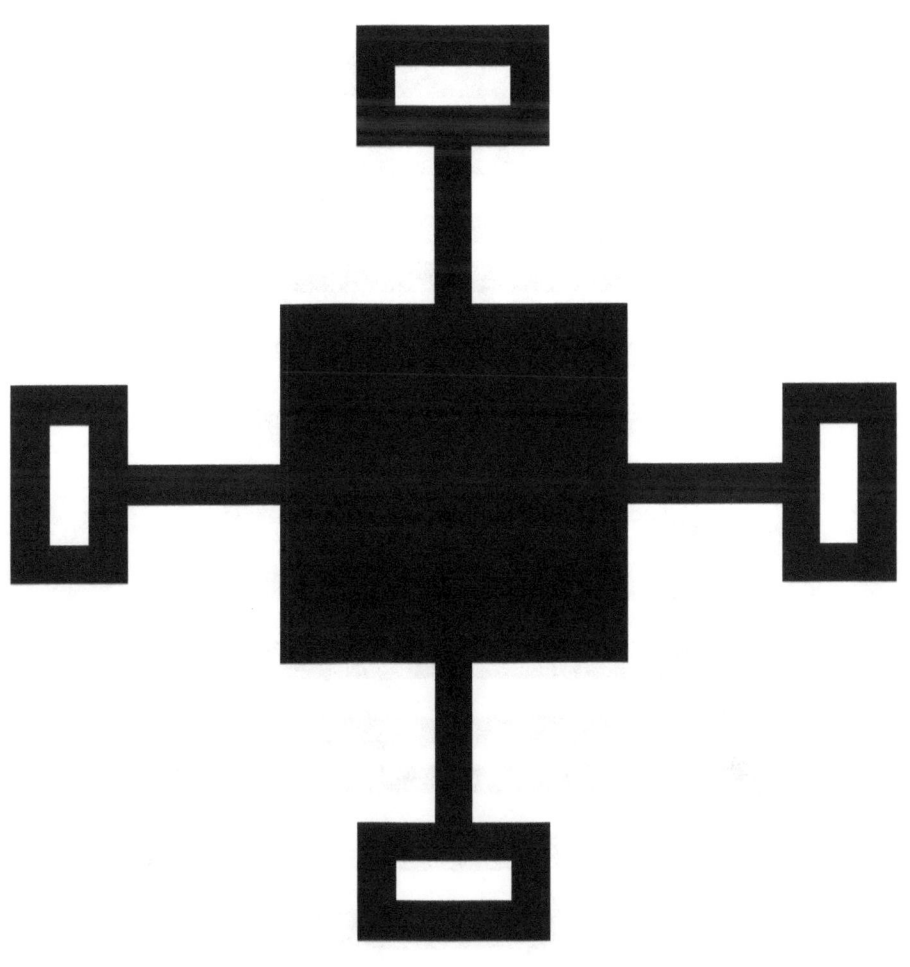

1,000,000 villages

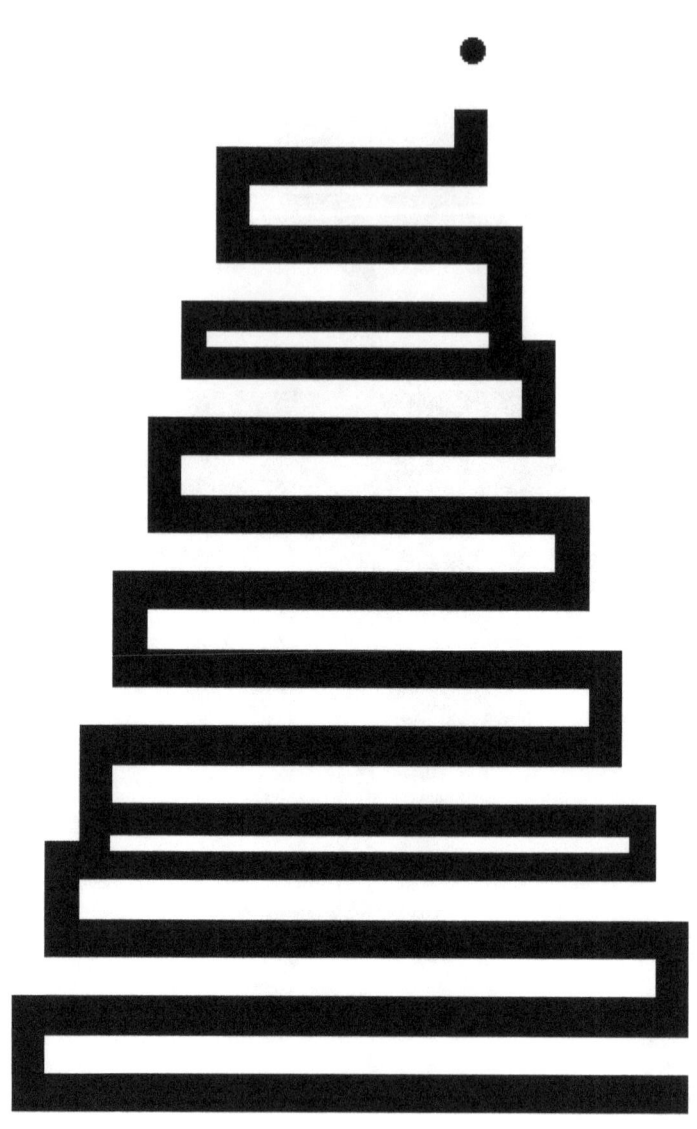

archivity

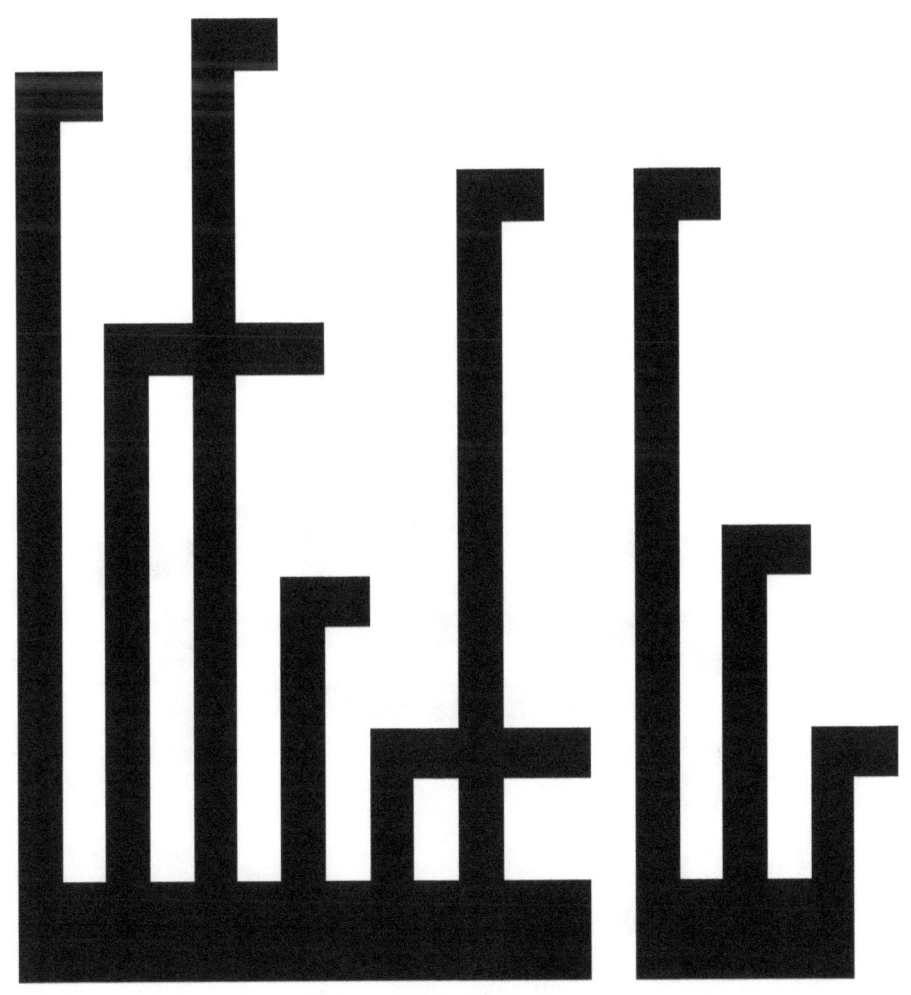

as ahead, so behind

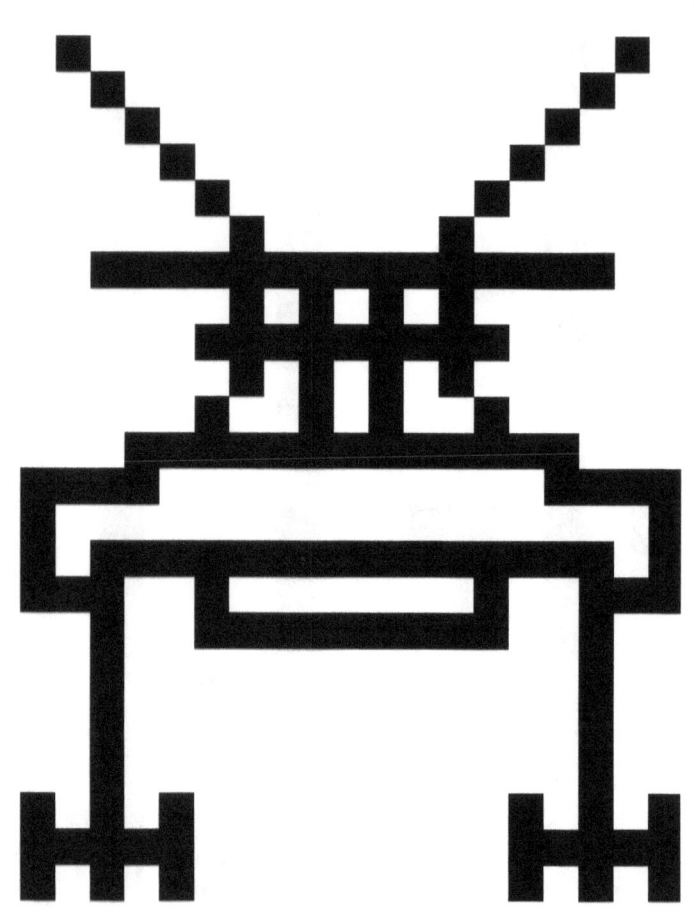

astral goat

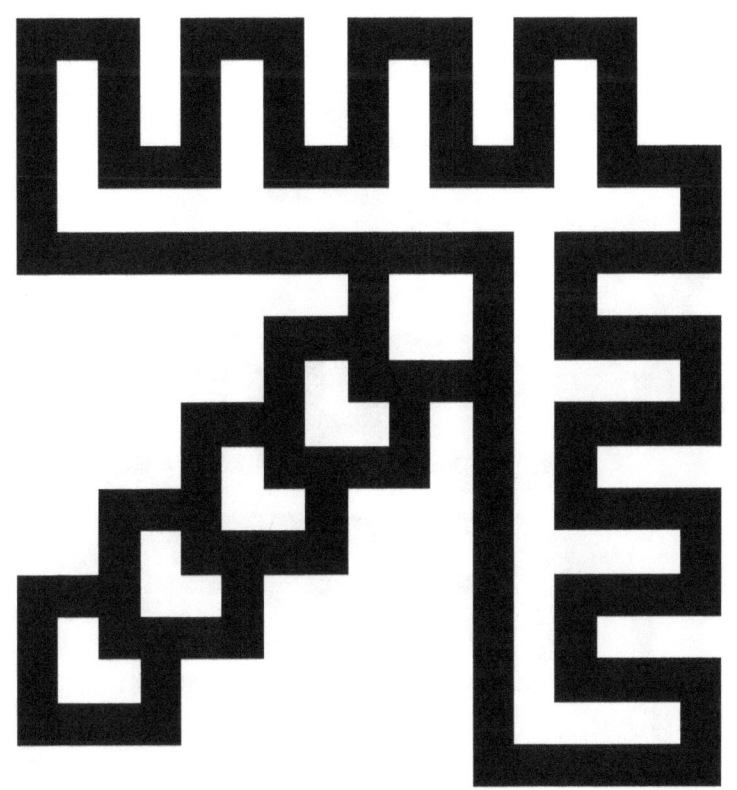

bibliostrophe

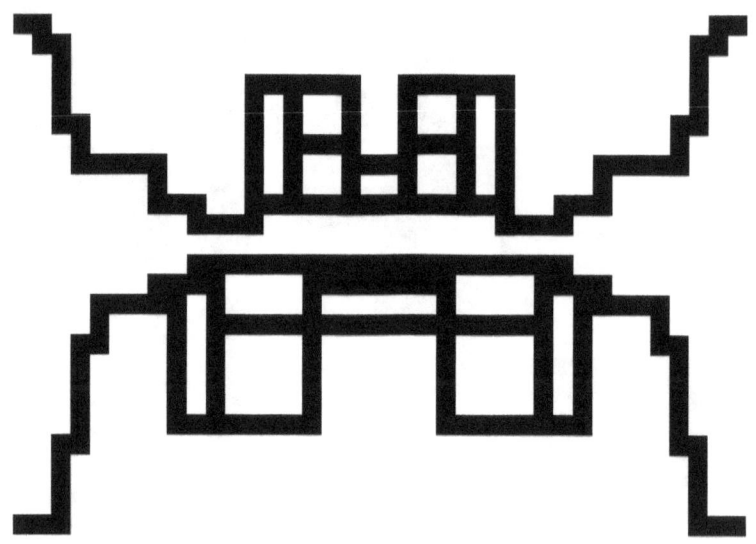

biopod

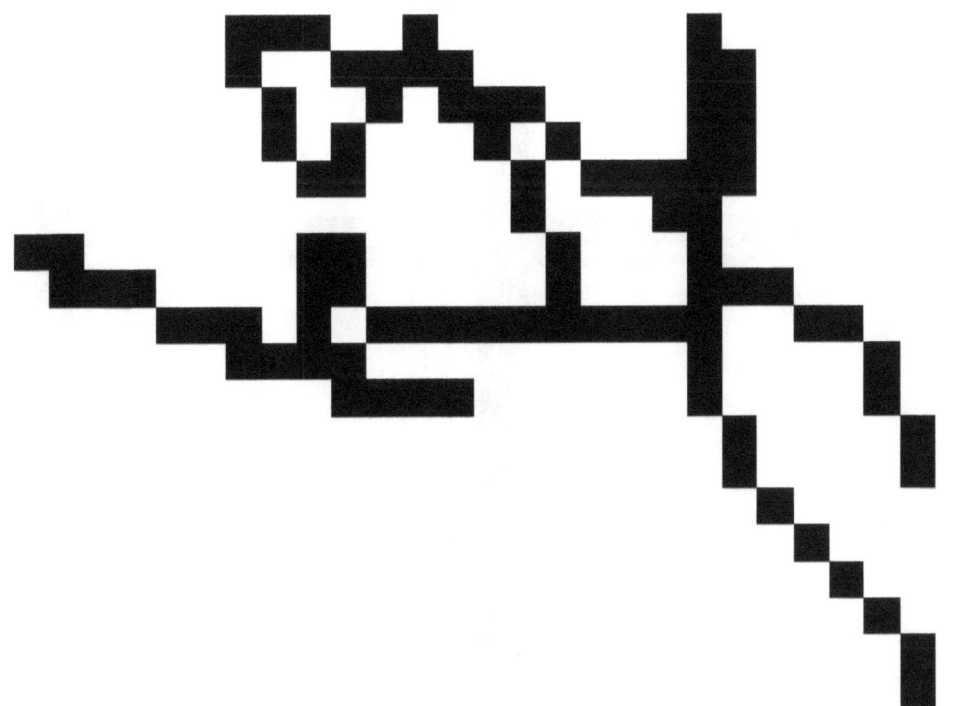

blurblock

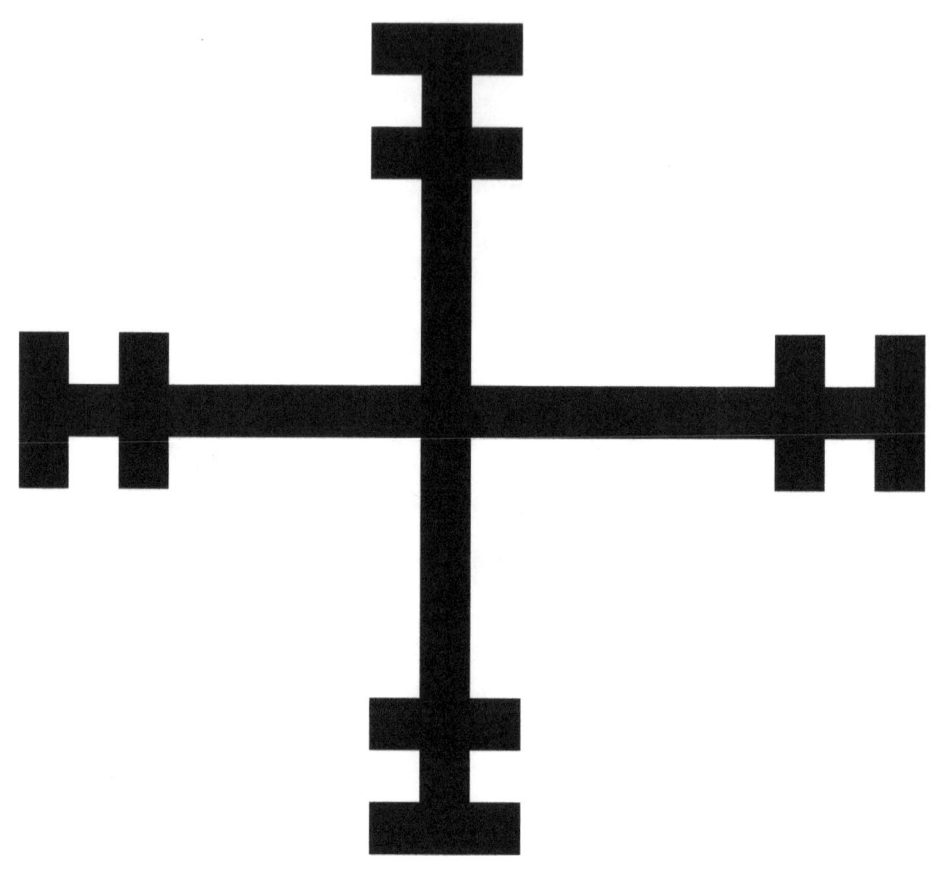

boaz

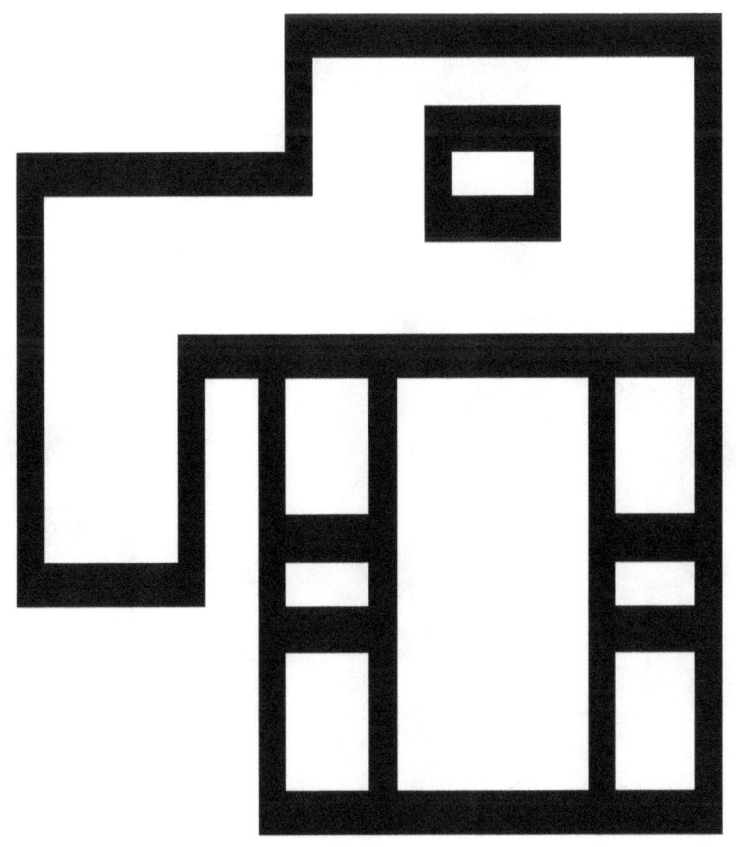

car

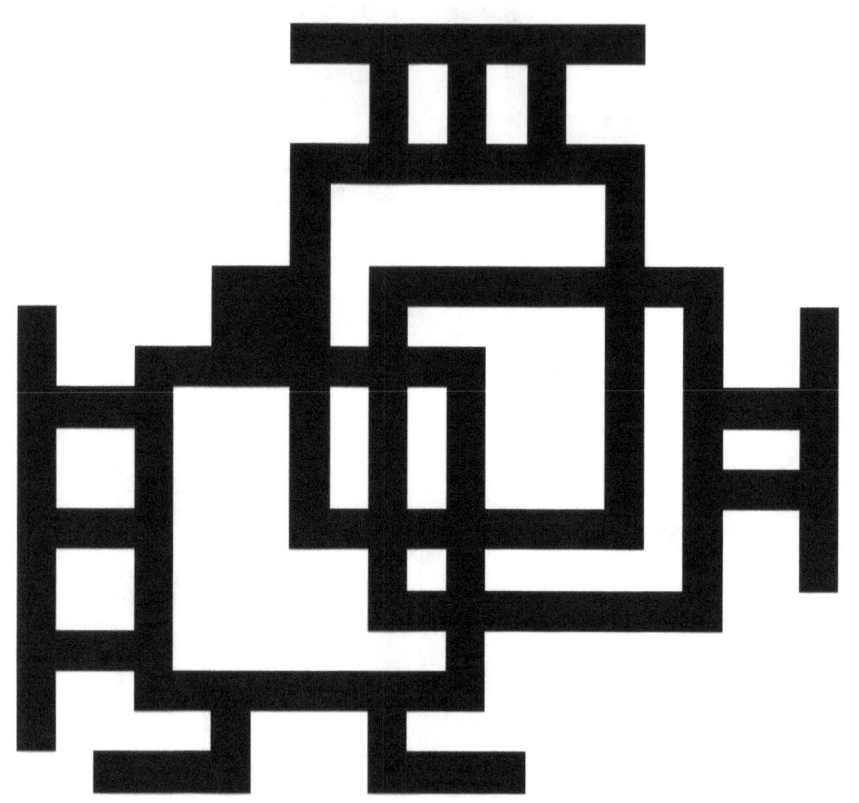

co-habitat

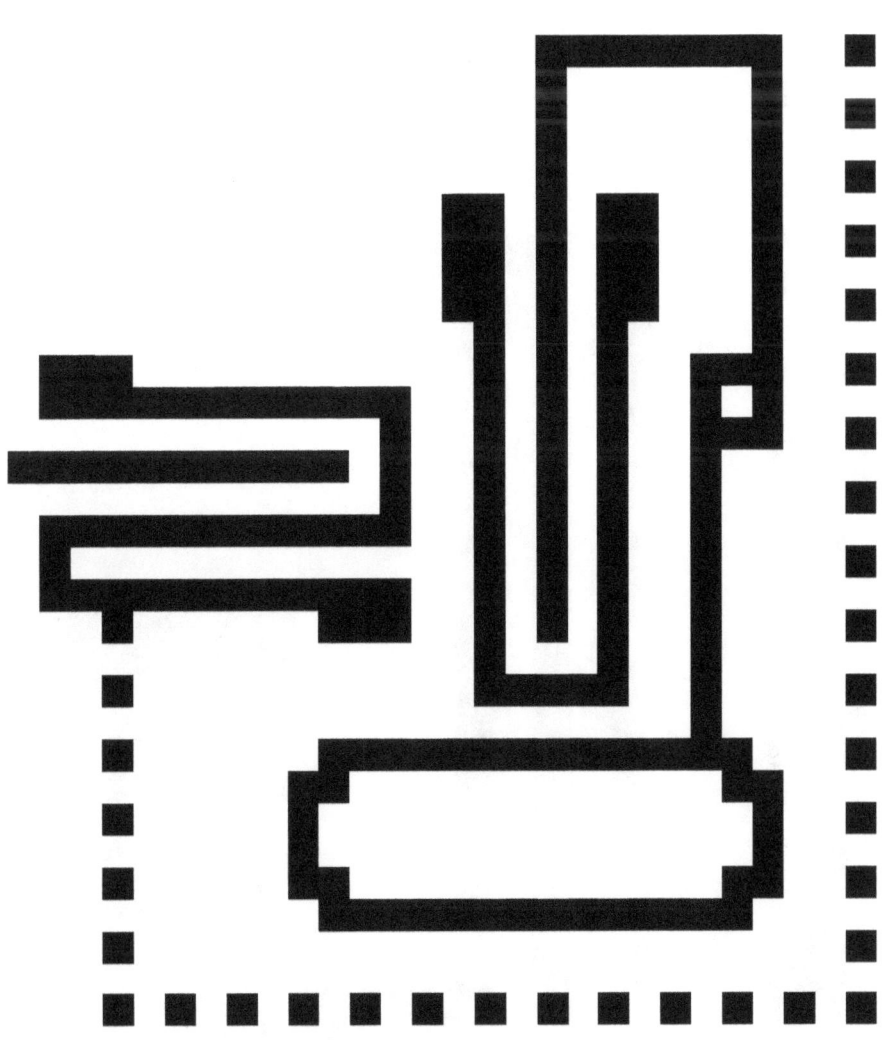

conversion

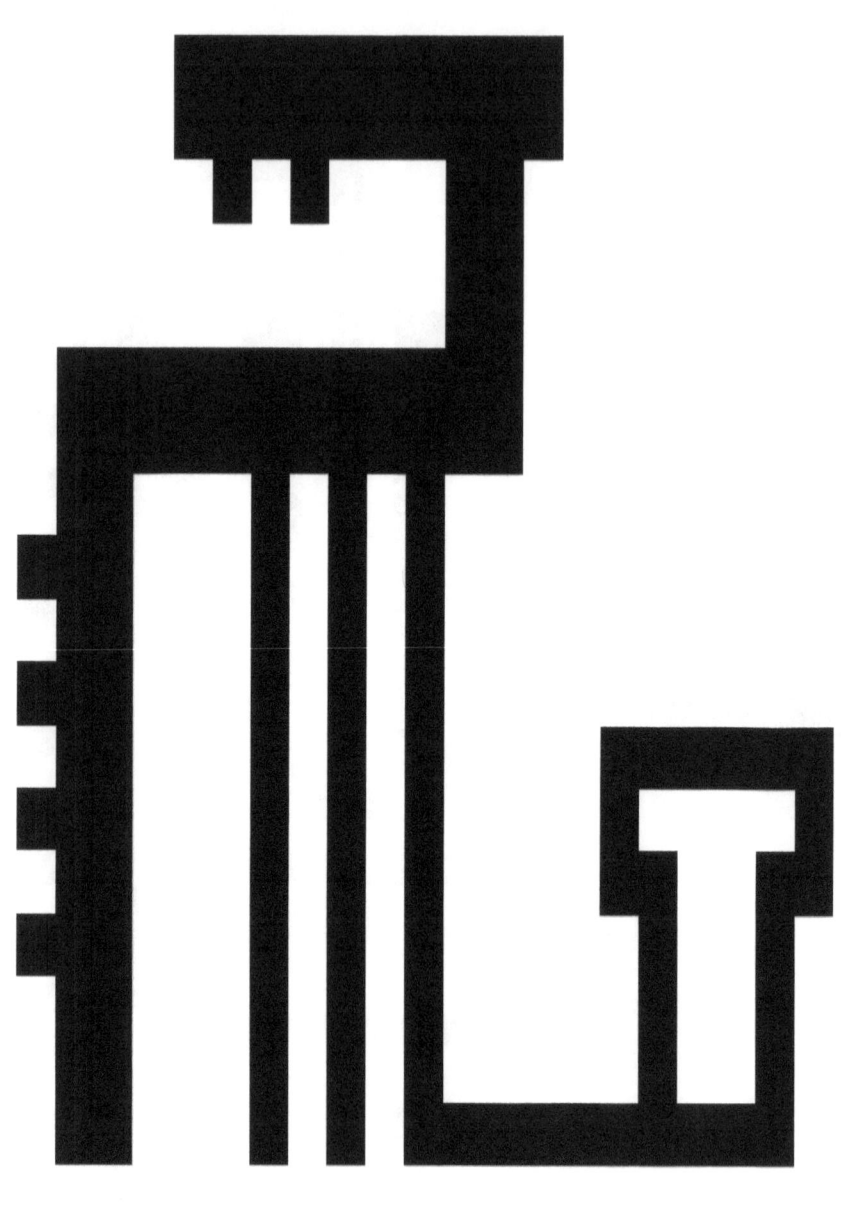

cultural placebo

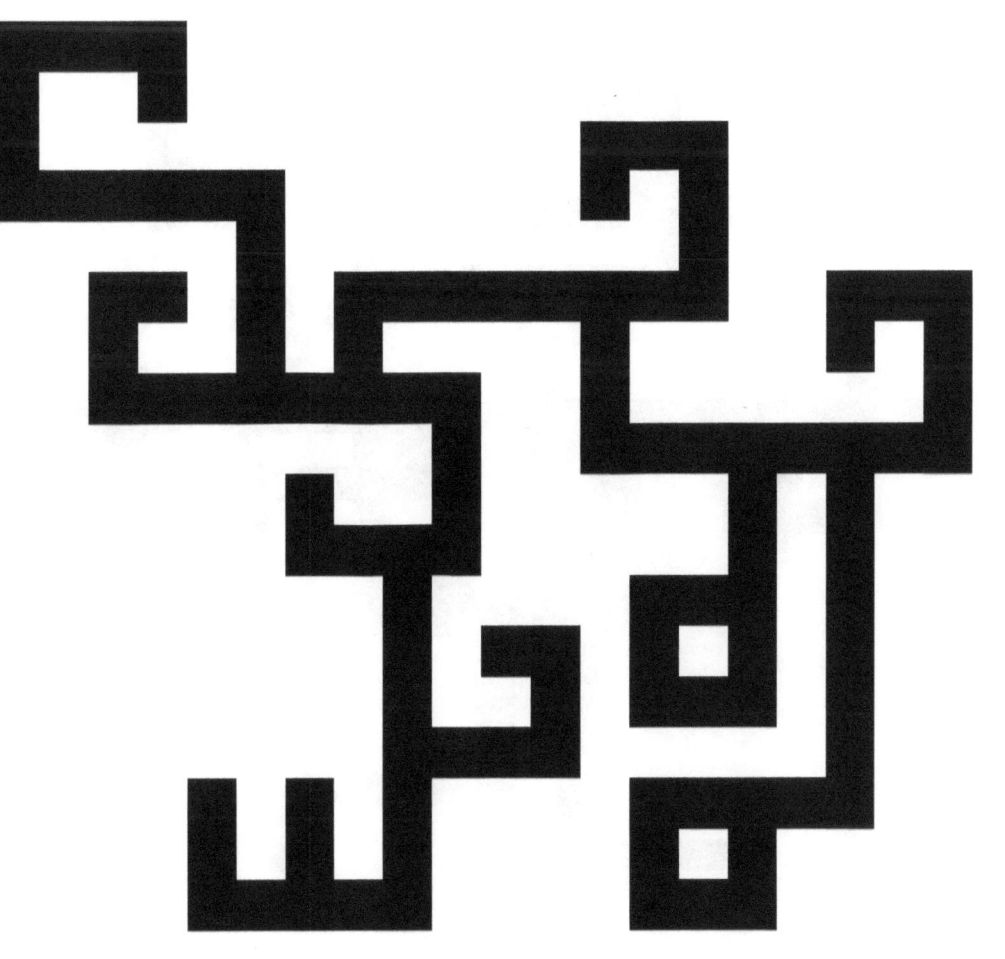

decentralized network

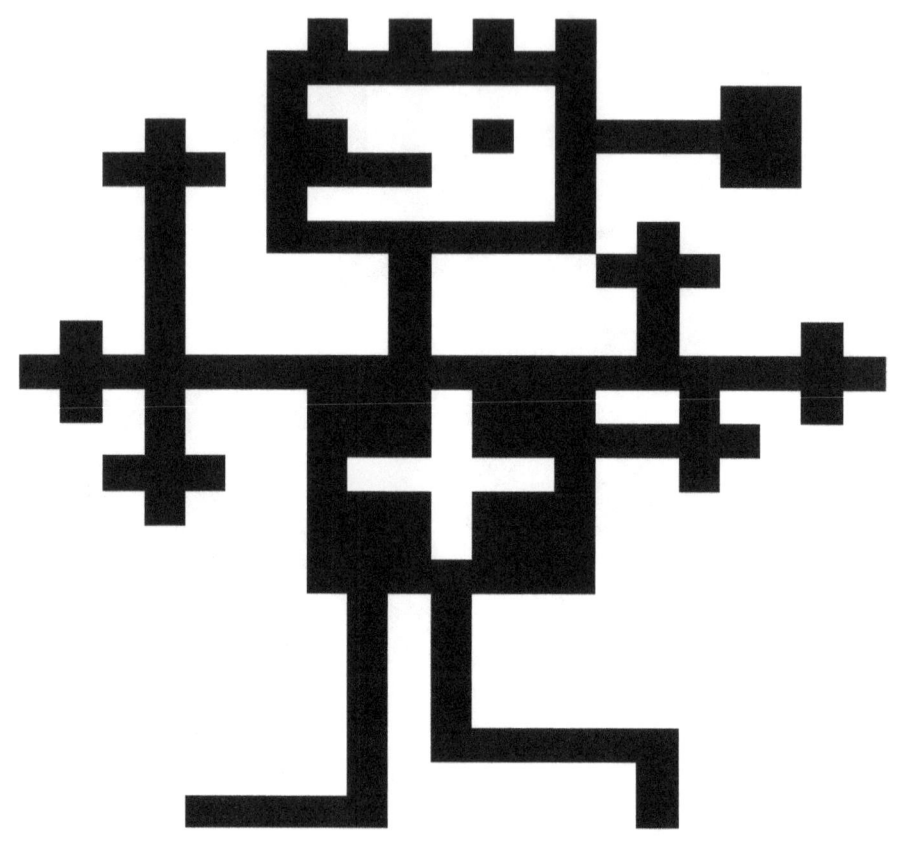

dreamtime post

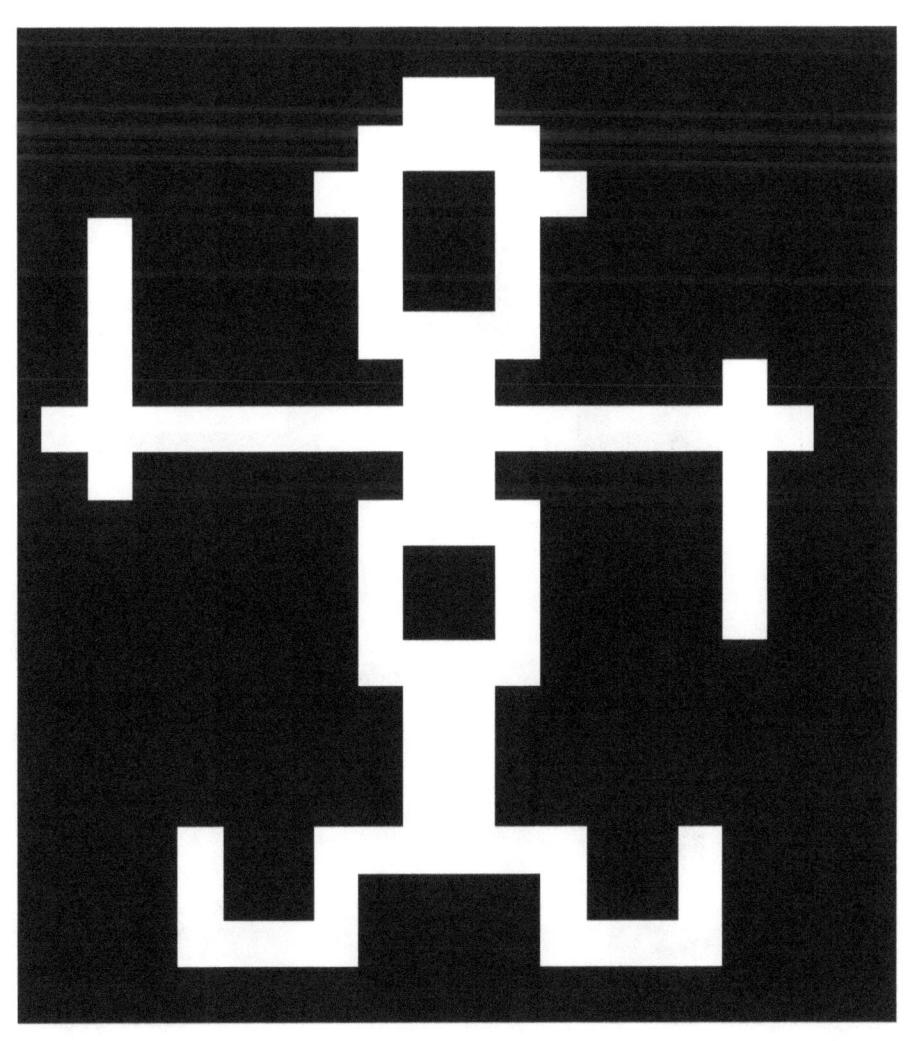

driftless permaculture

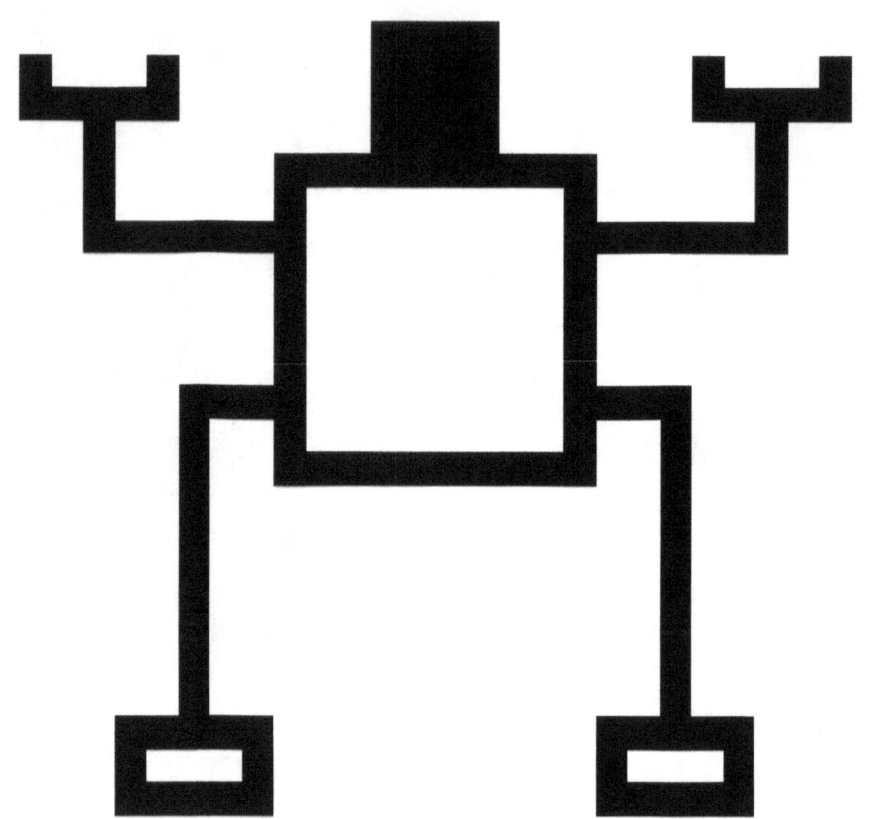

drop dance

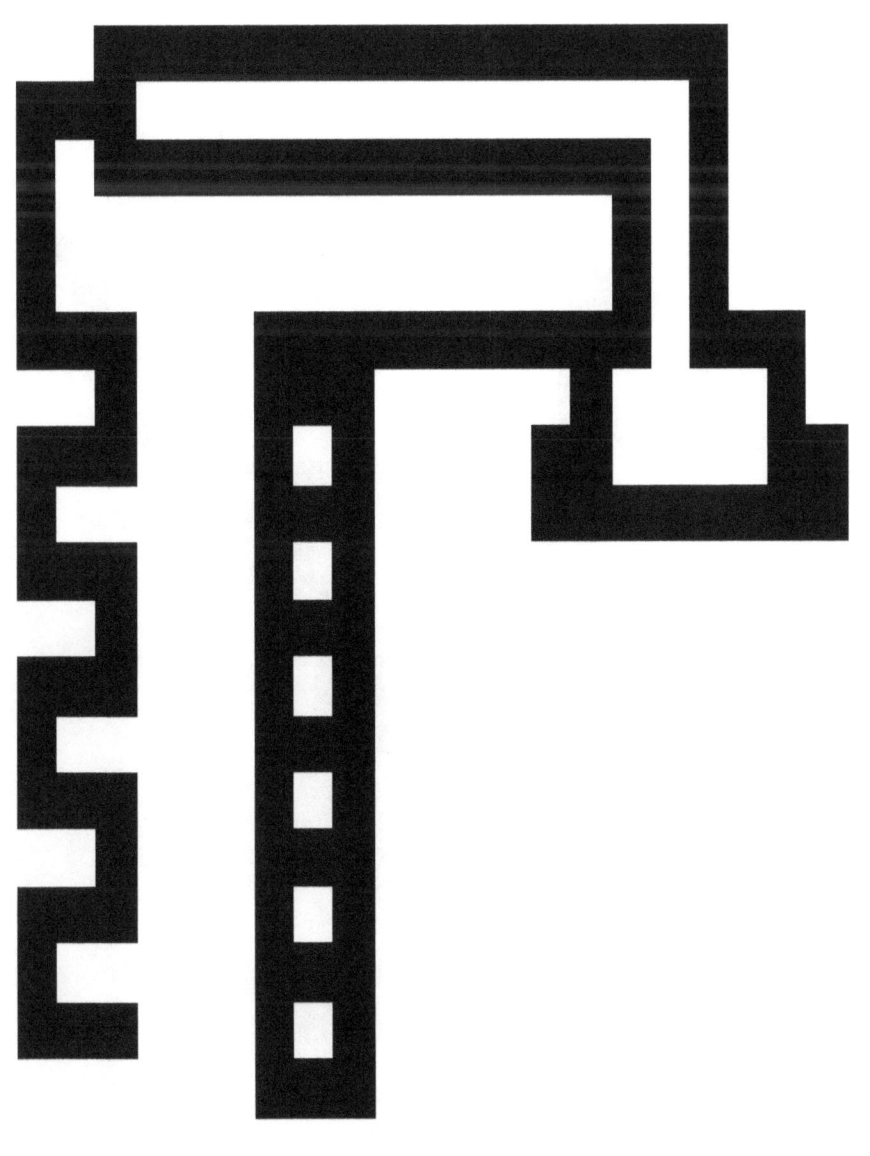

dzly

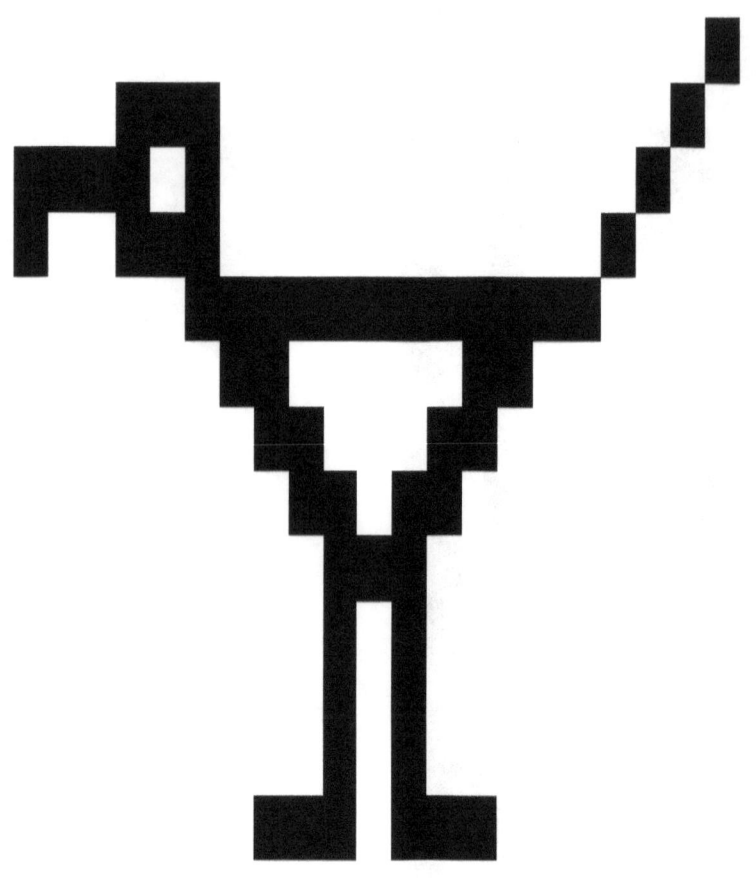

endangered

18

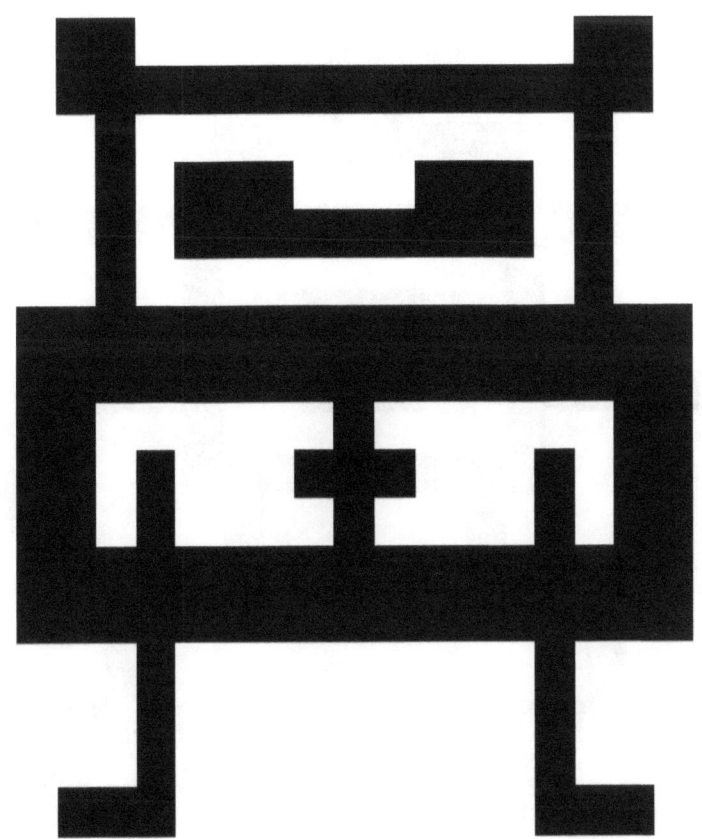

gibber

19

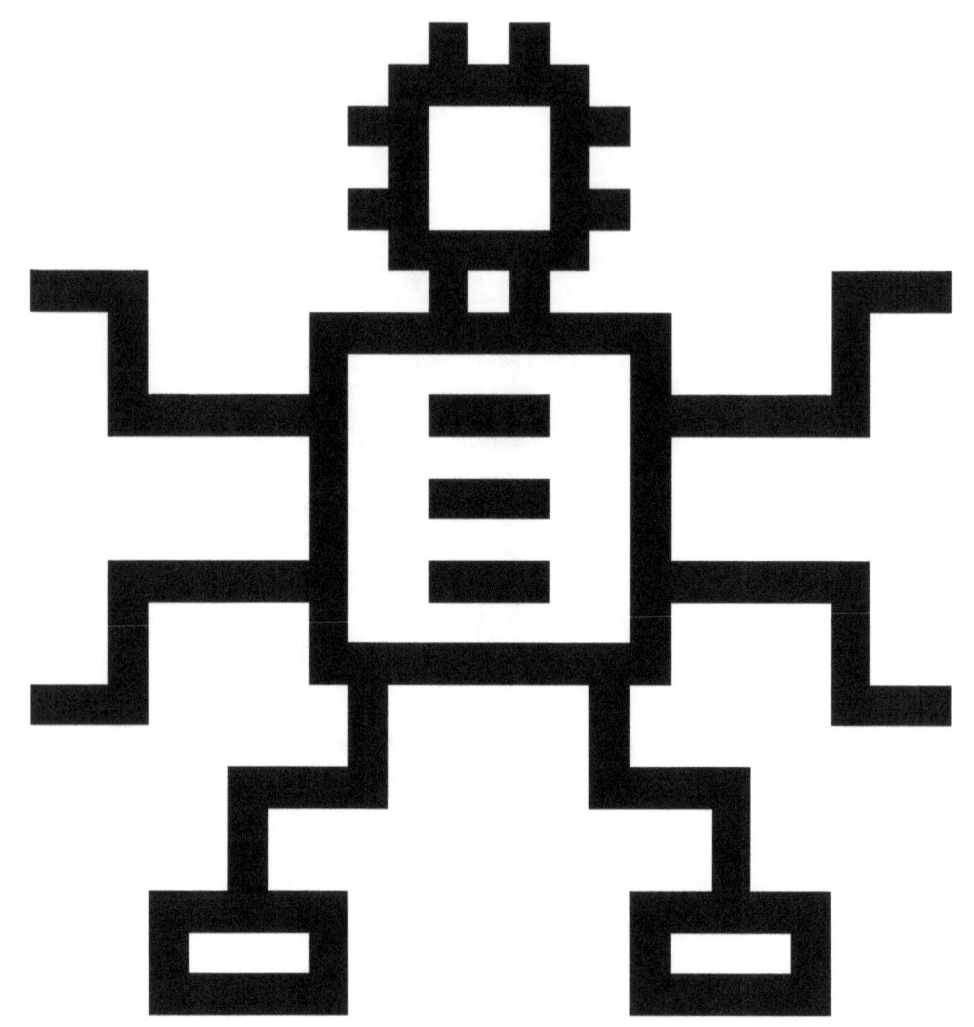

glue belly

goddess

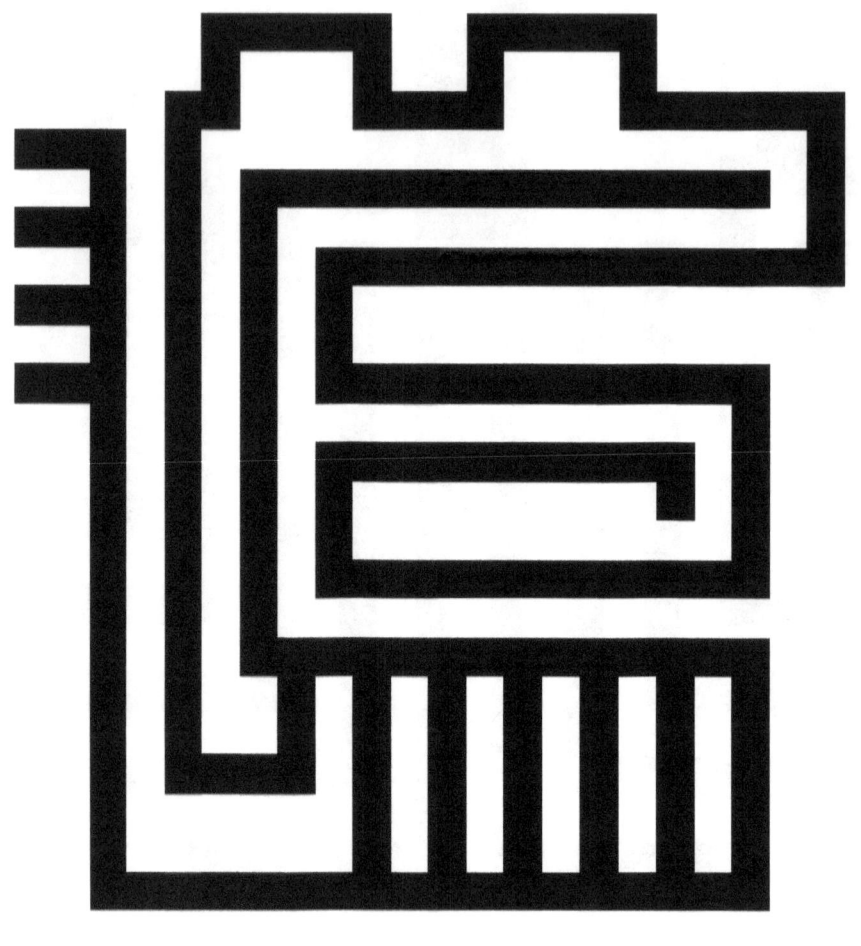

grow soil

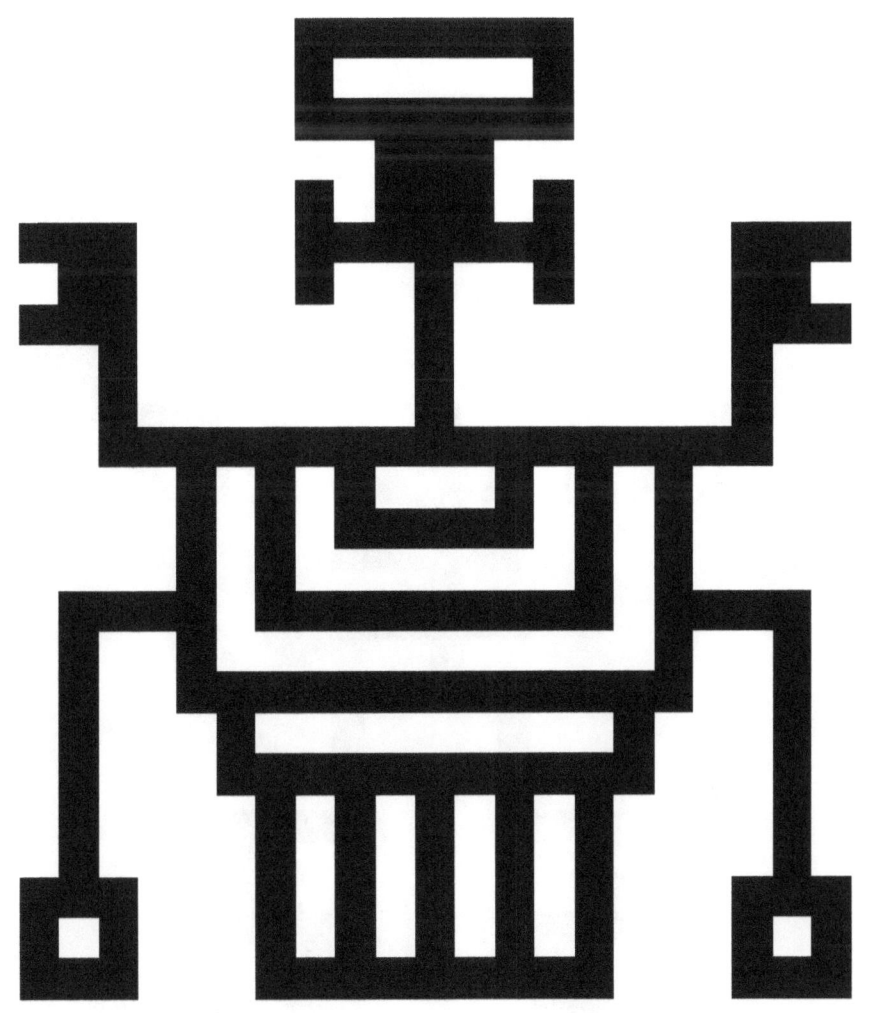

hacker

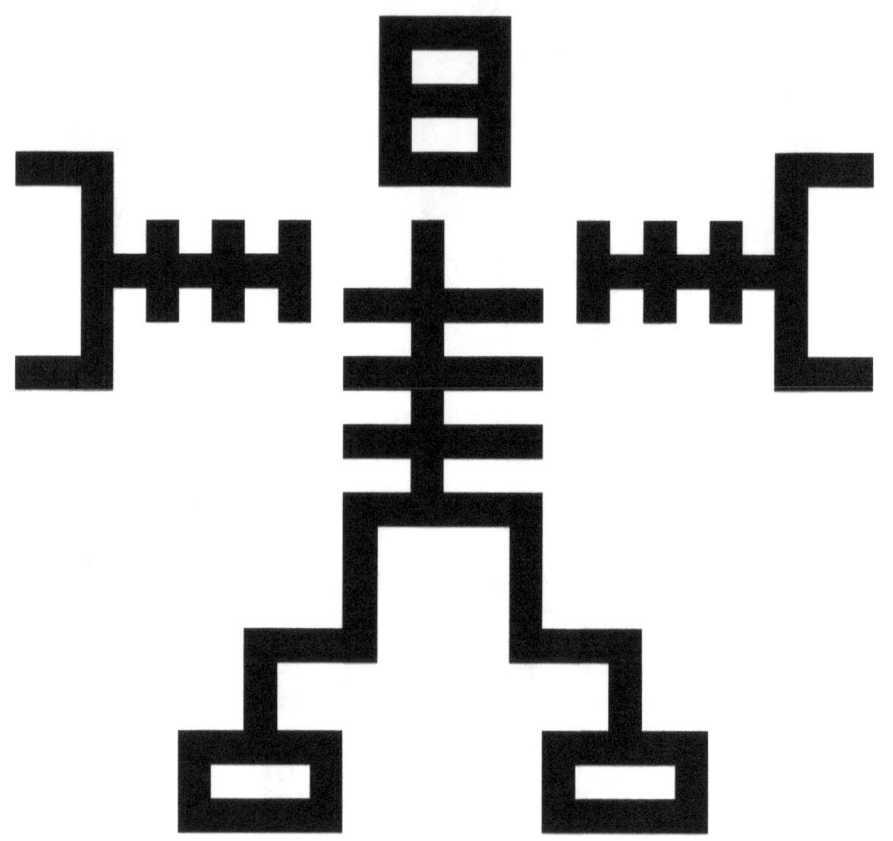

home zoom

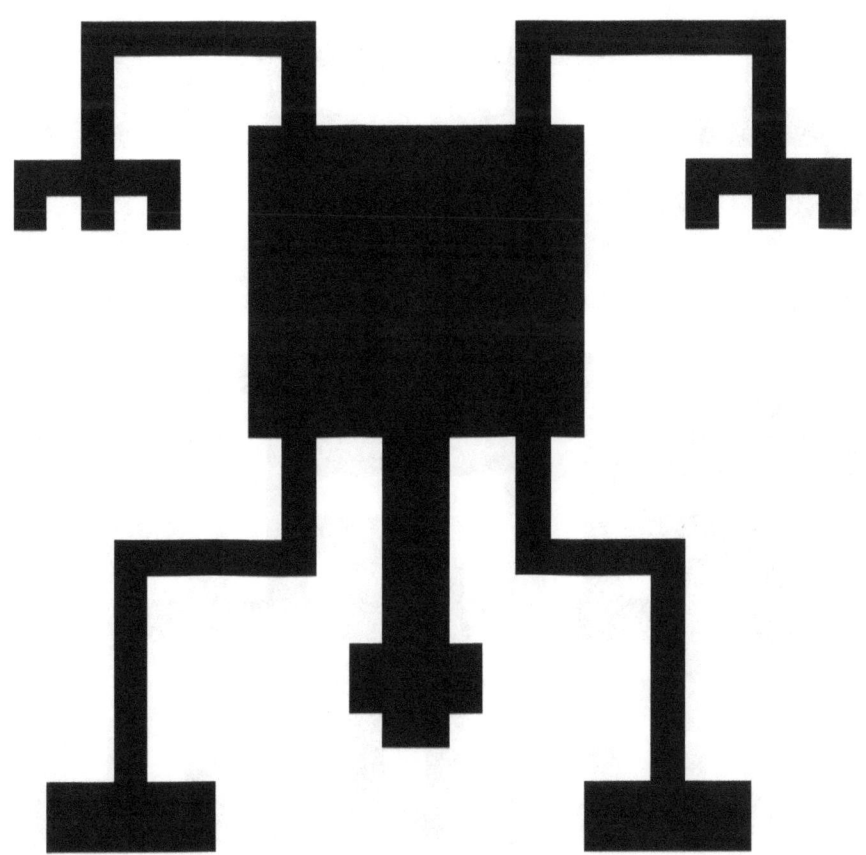

hump dance

hyper network

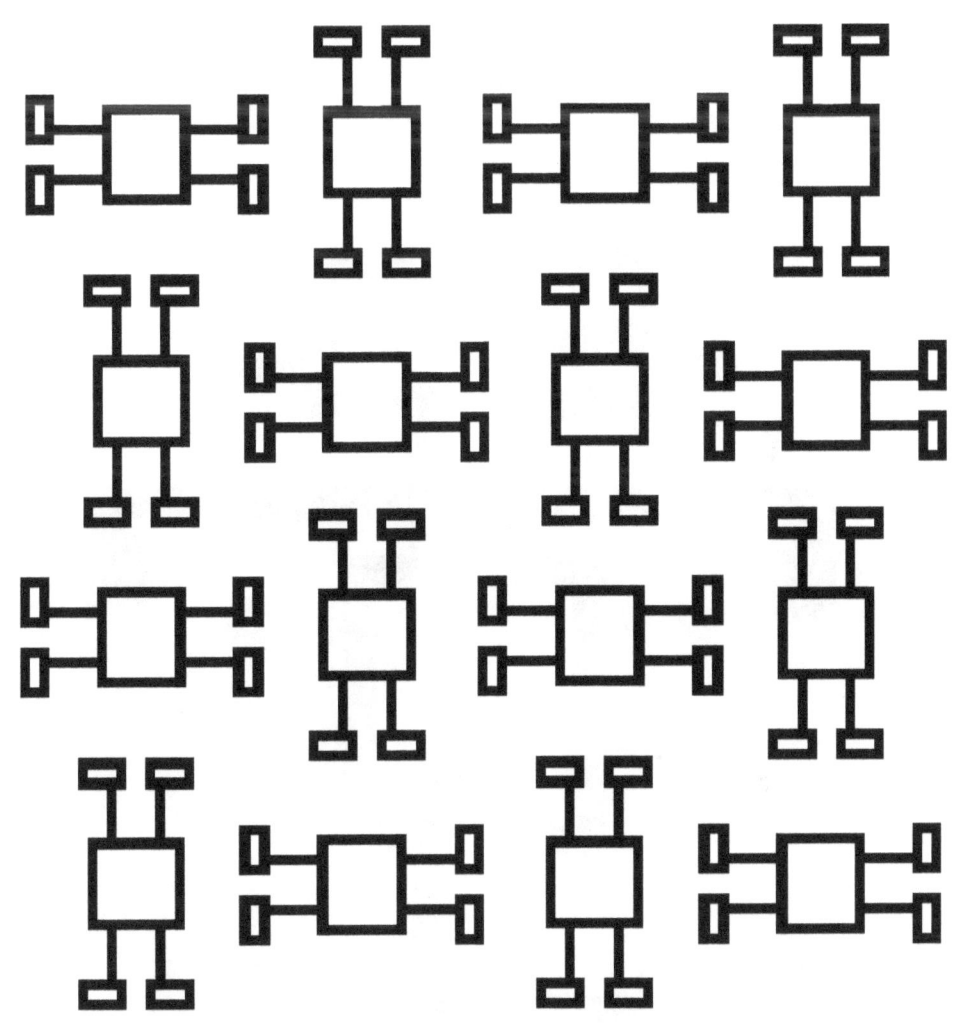

hyperkulture

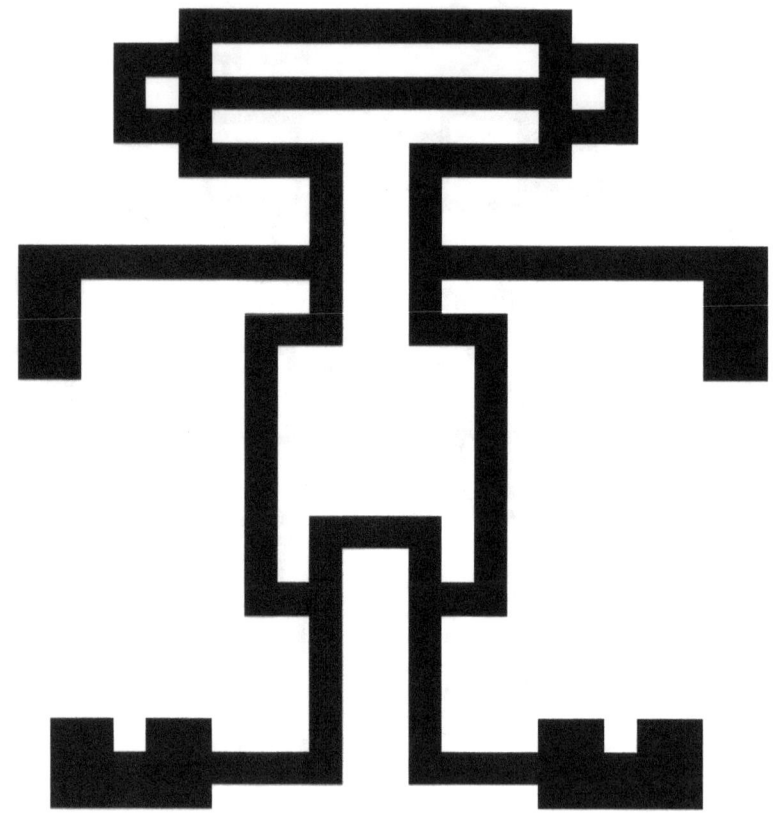

inkling

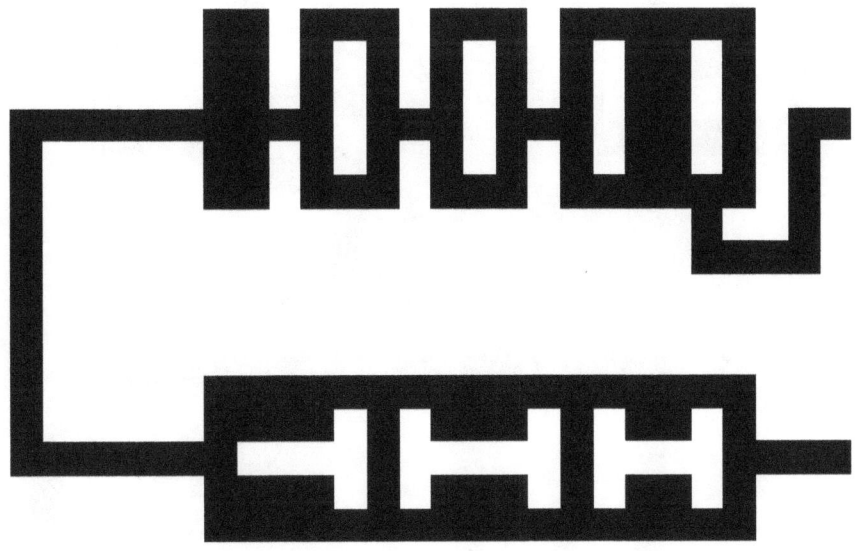

limit

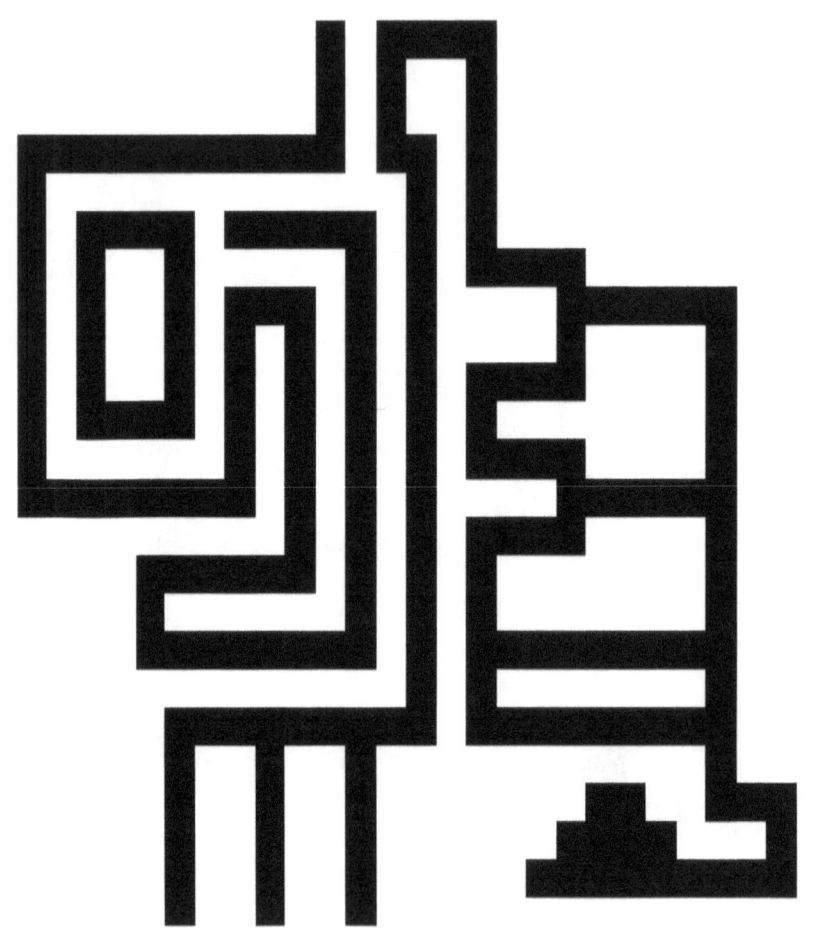

magniwisdom

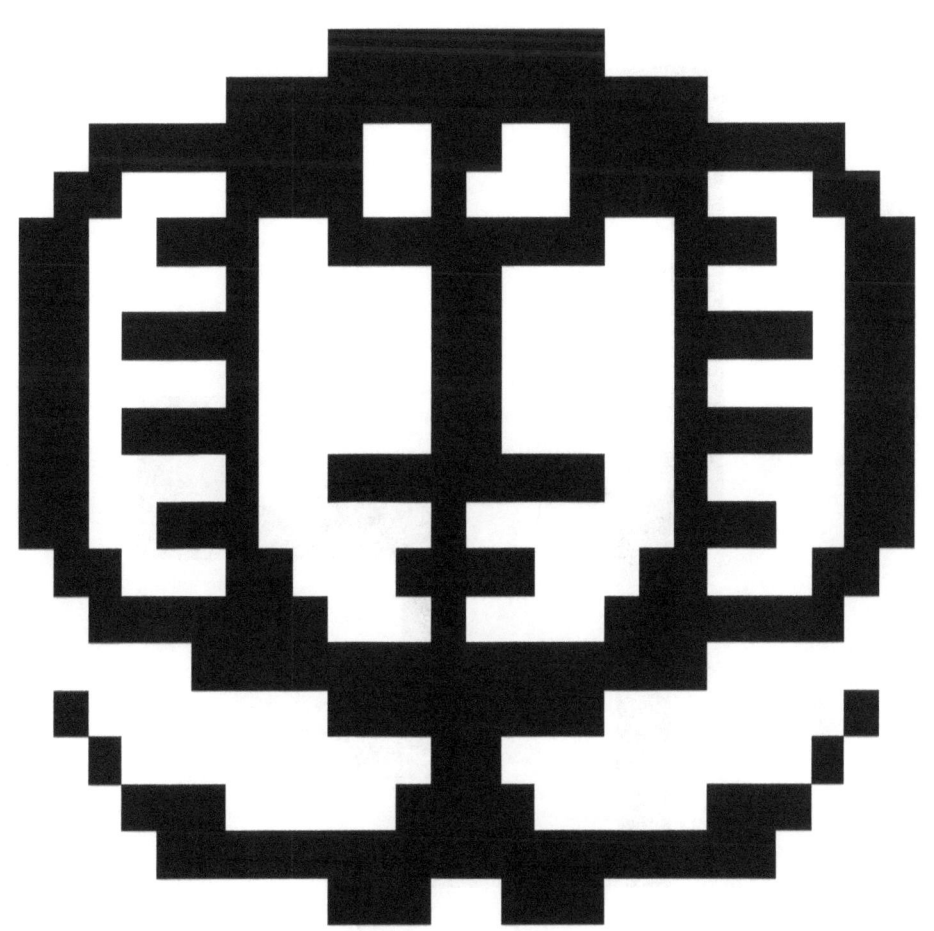

merkaka

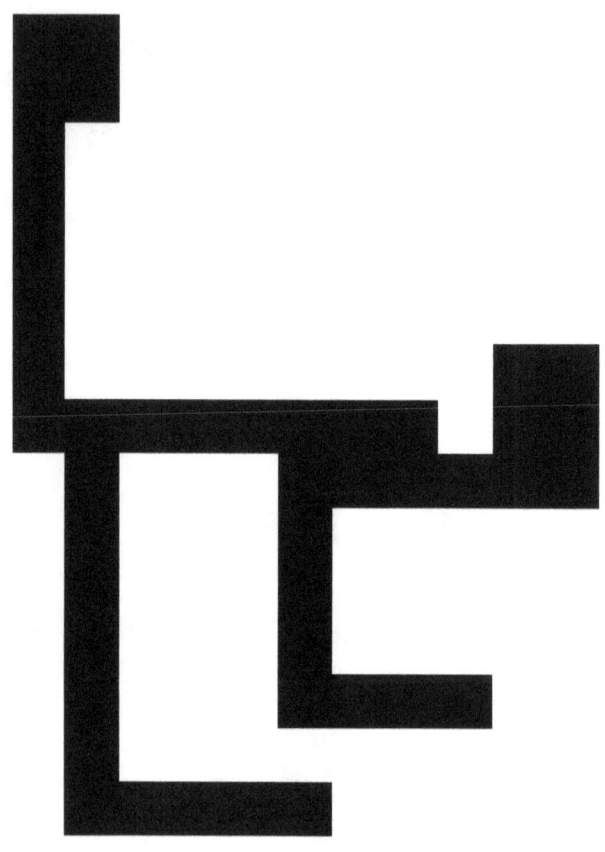

monkeyback

Mr Ink

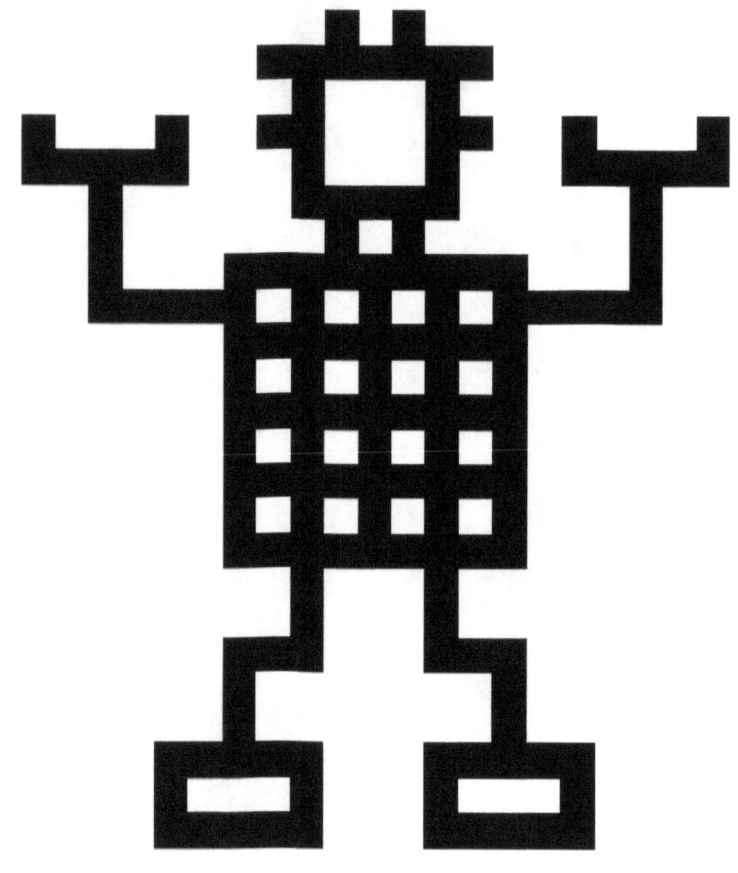

multi-task environment

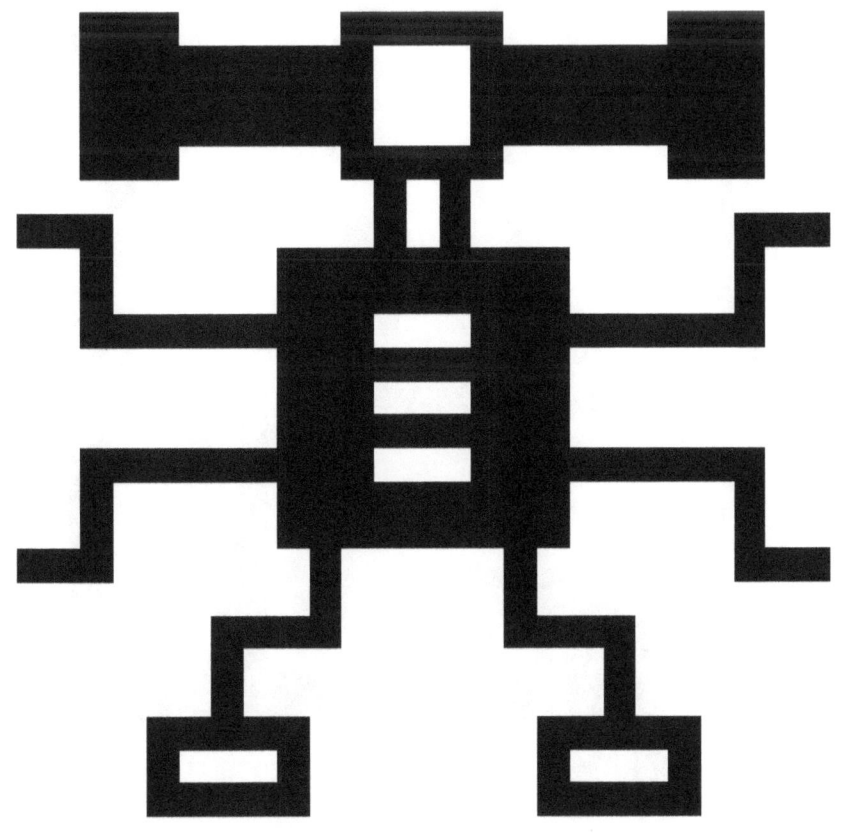

nail head

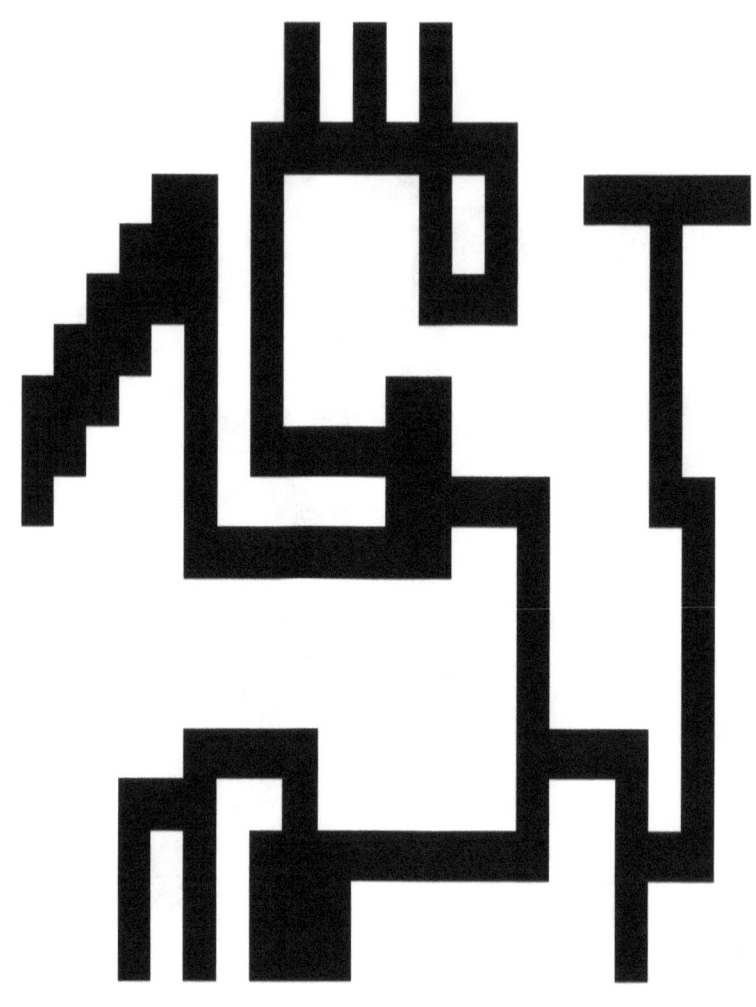

noisecore

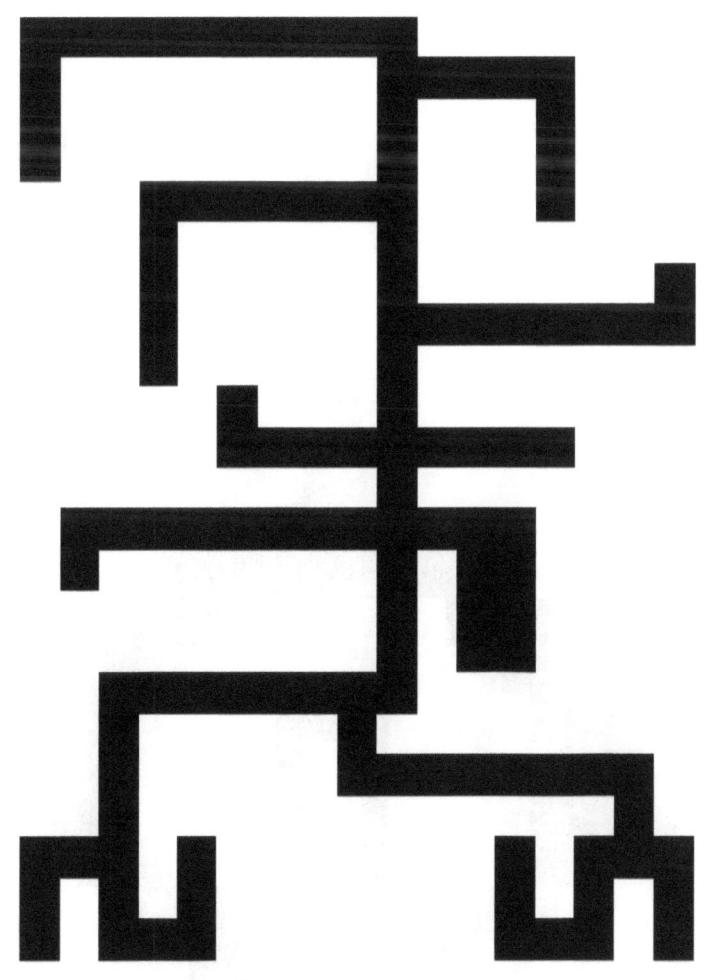

nomadic

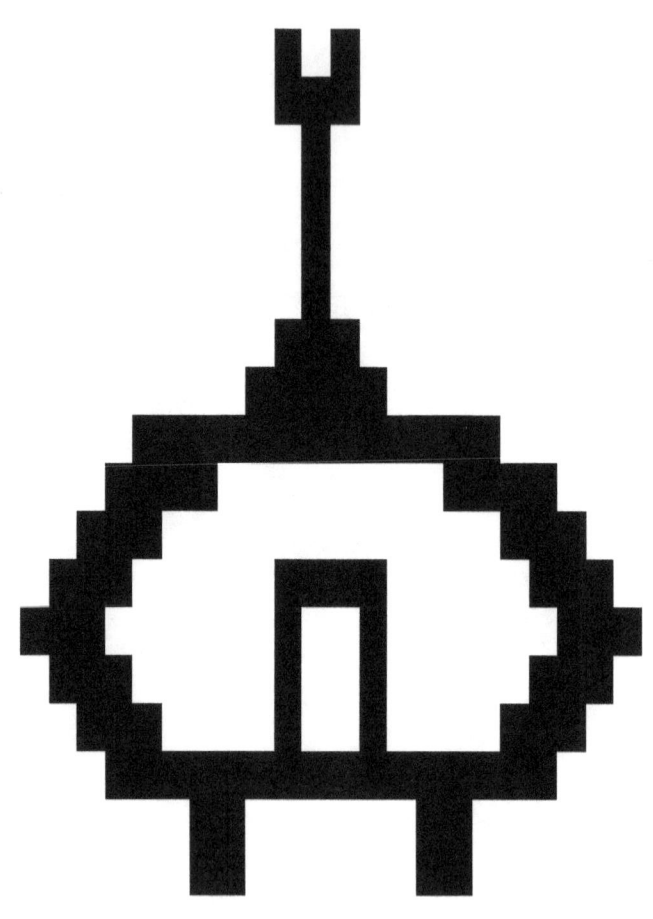

not a flying saucer

38

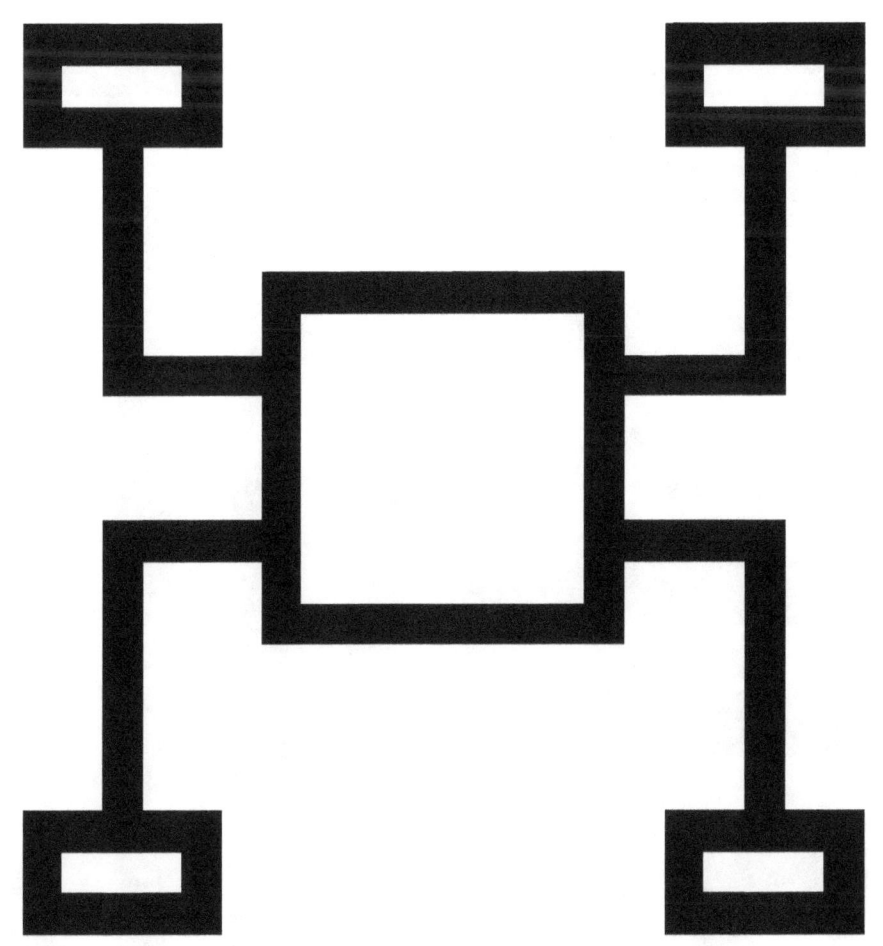

remedy

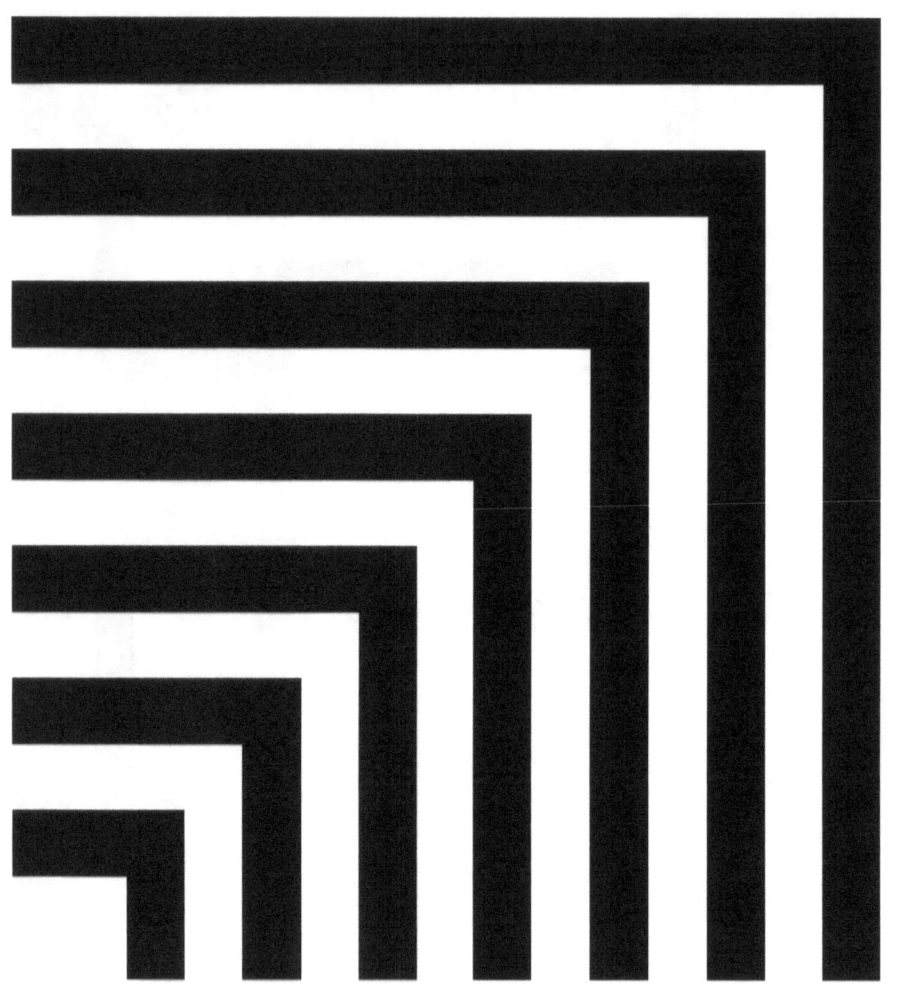

SASE

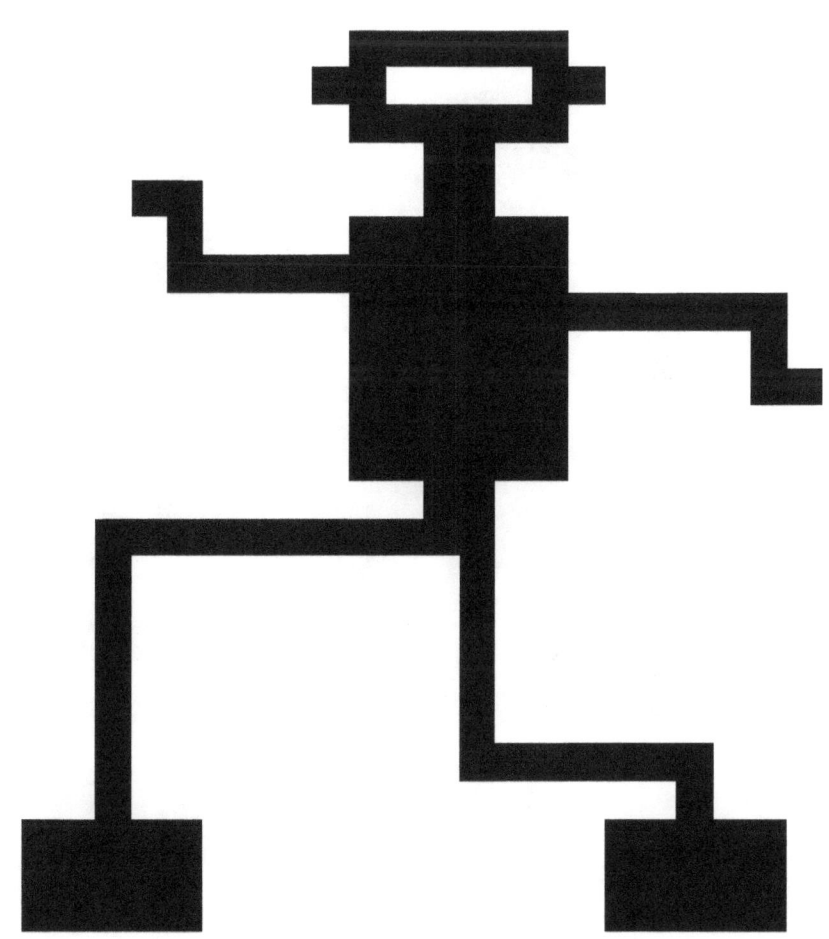

seek & ye

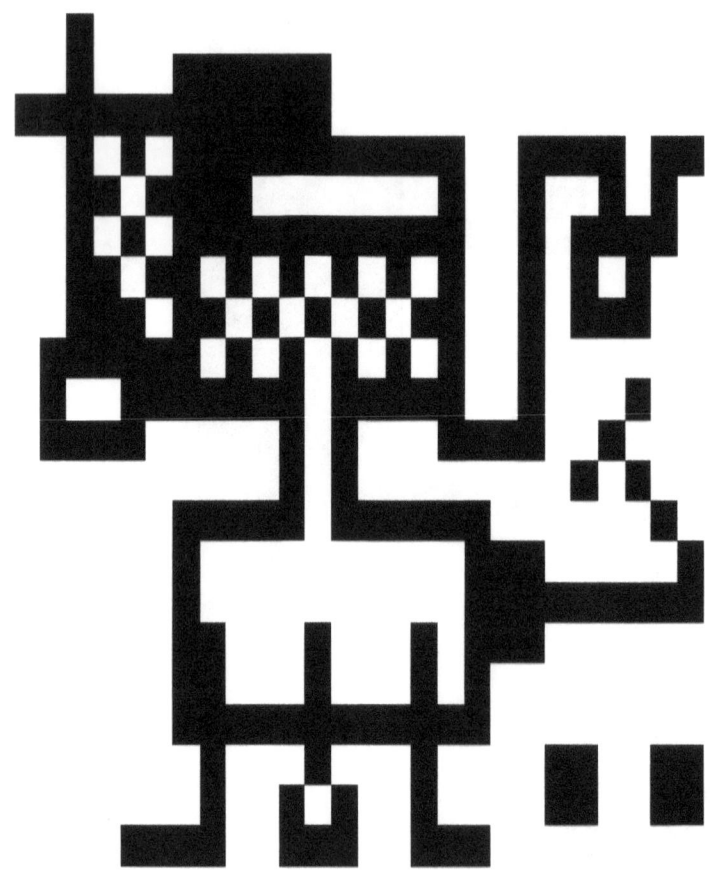

skattled

42

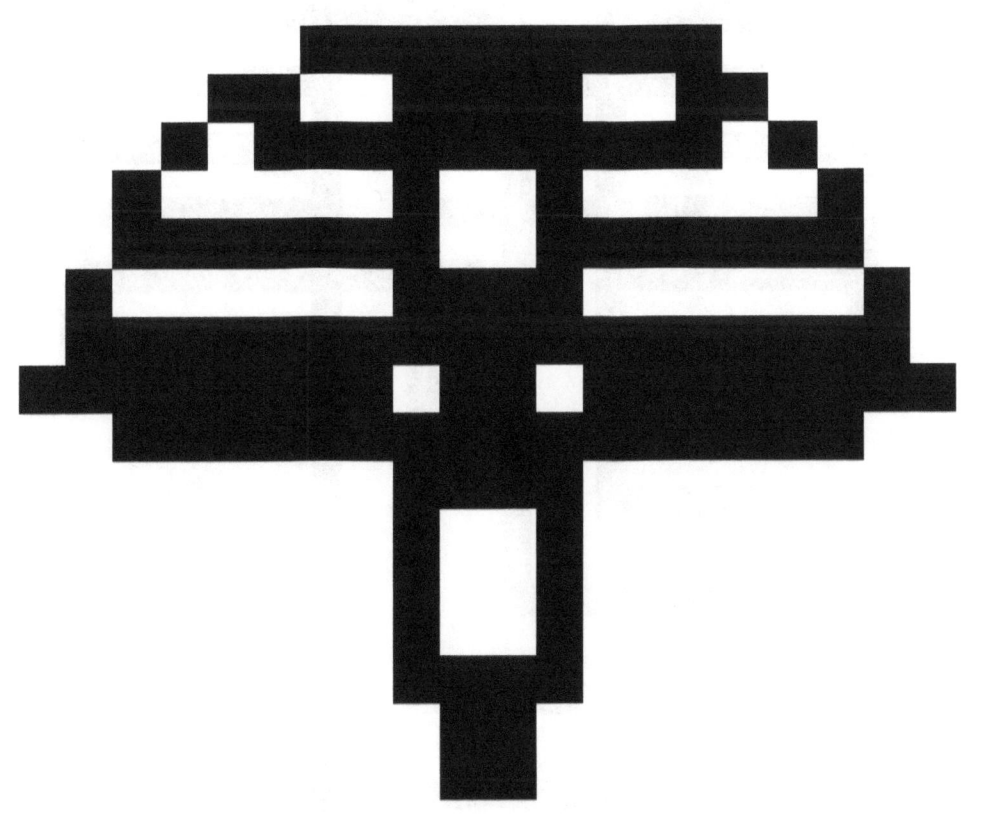

spore plug

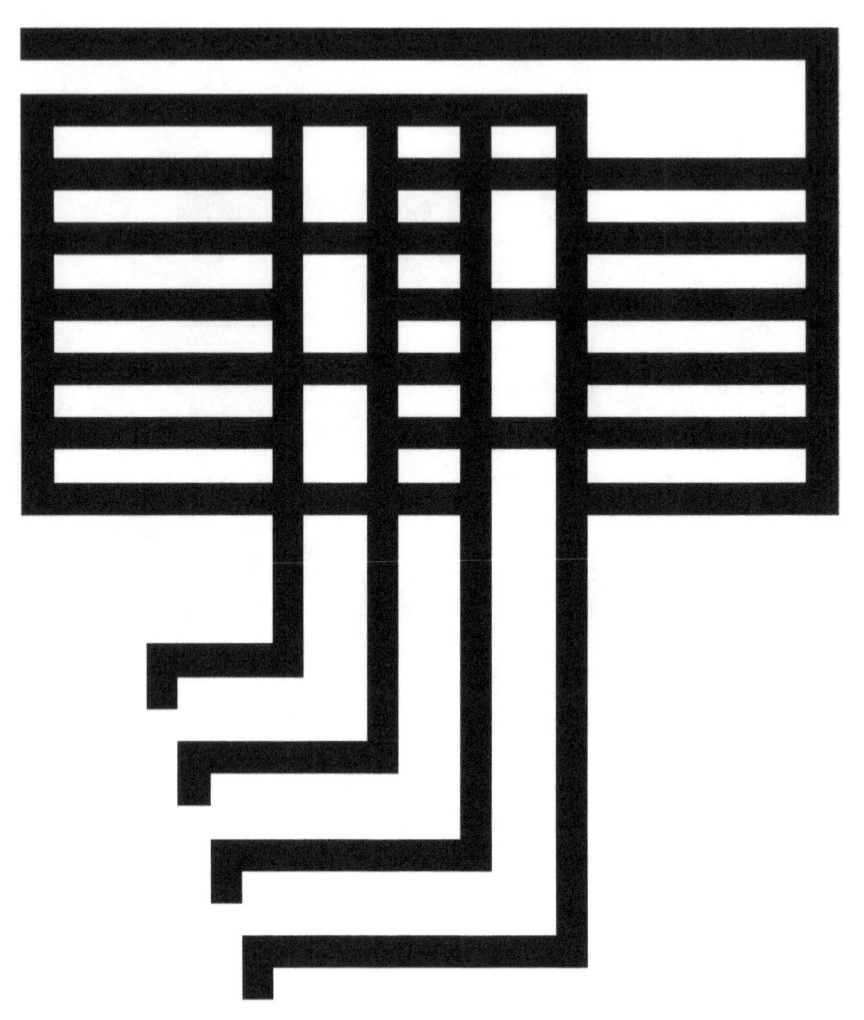

turtle phone

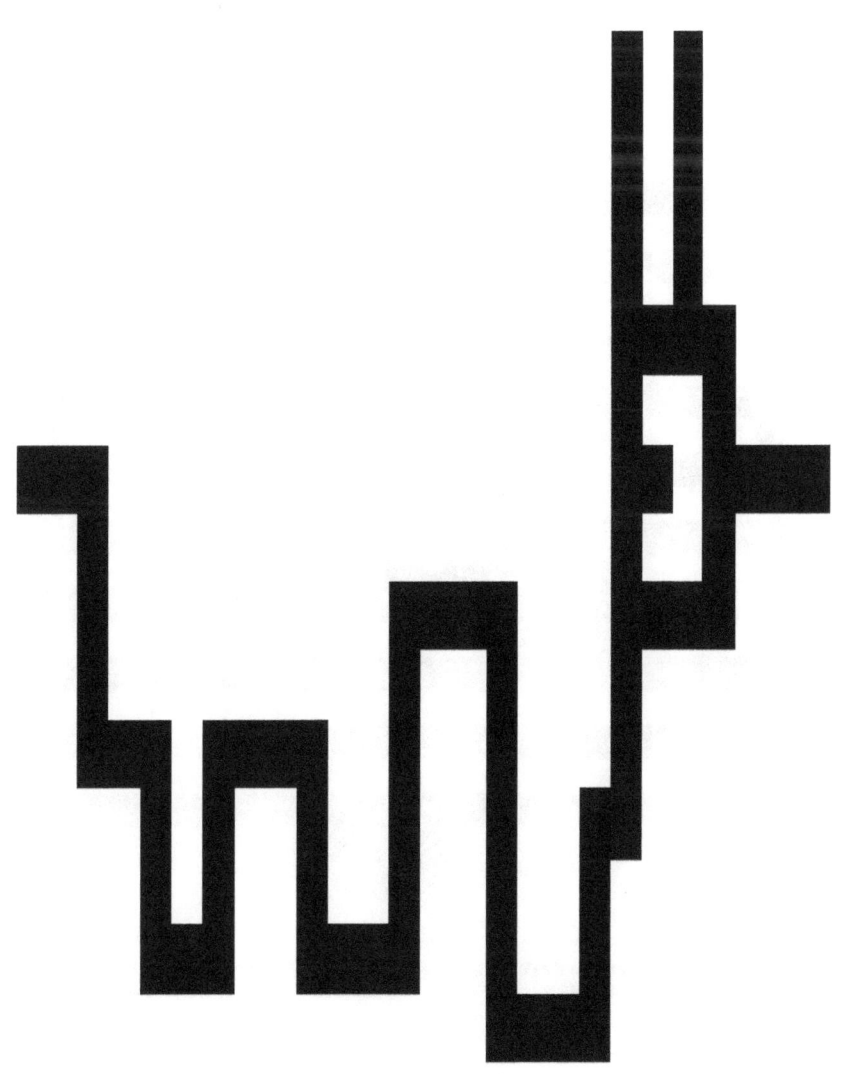

ur-ka-mik

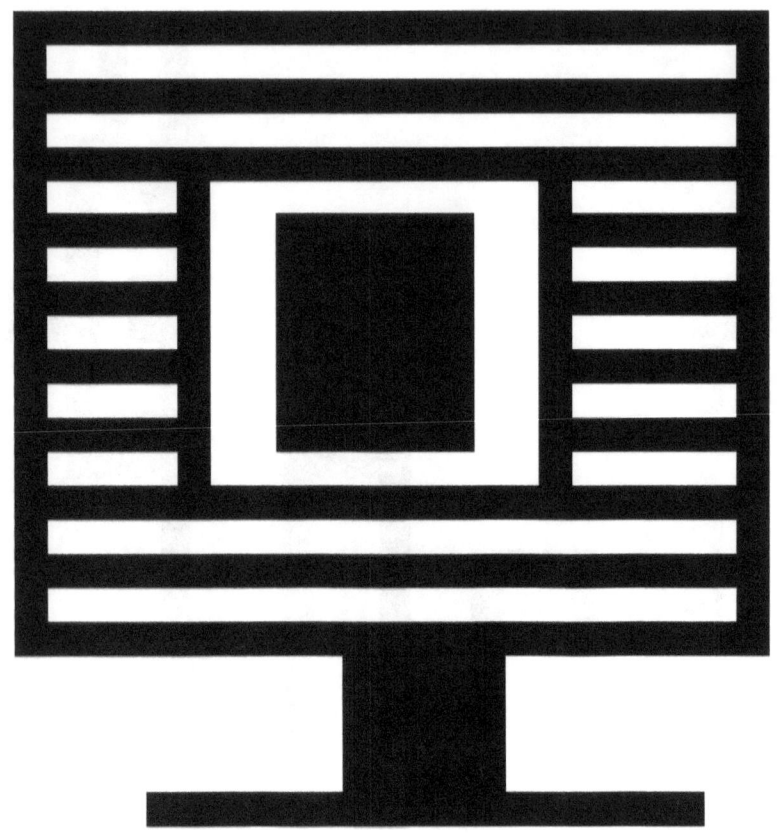

zaum TV

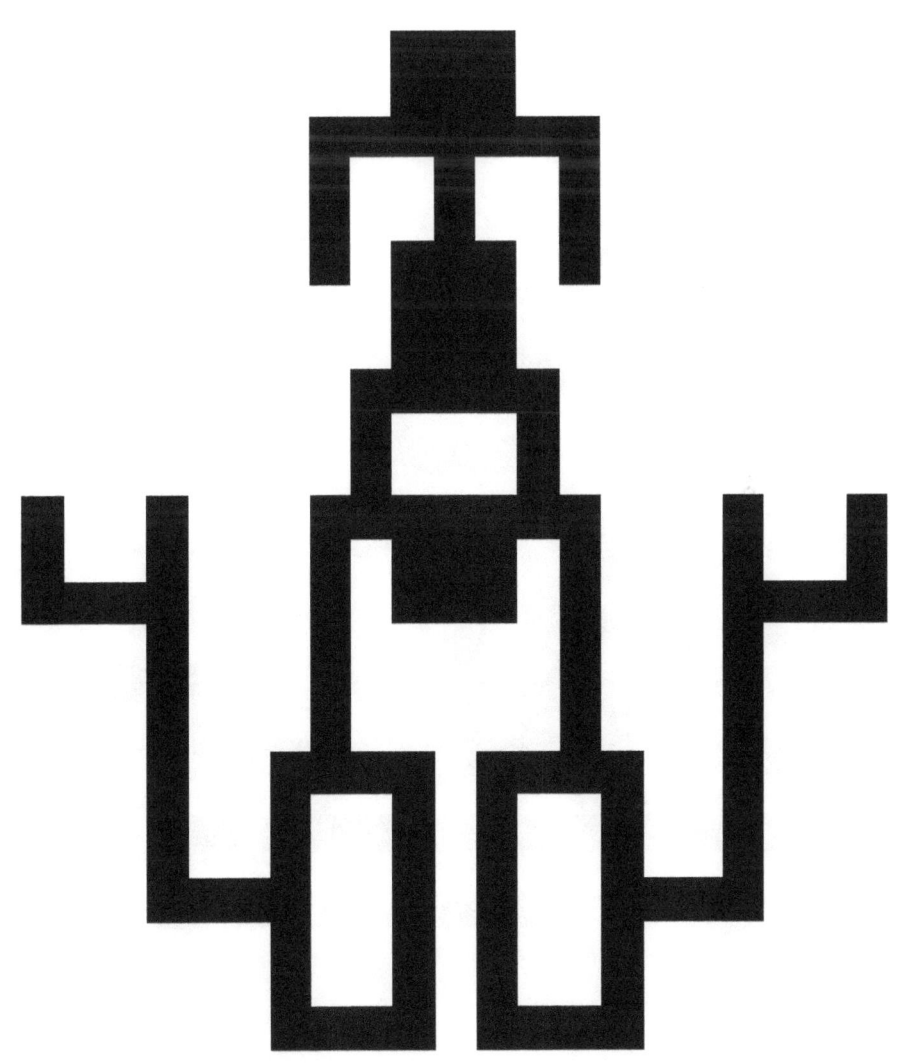

zingtut

47

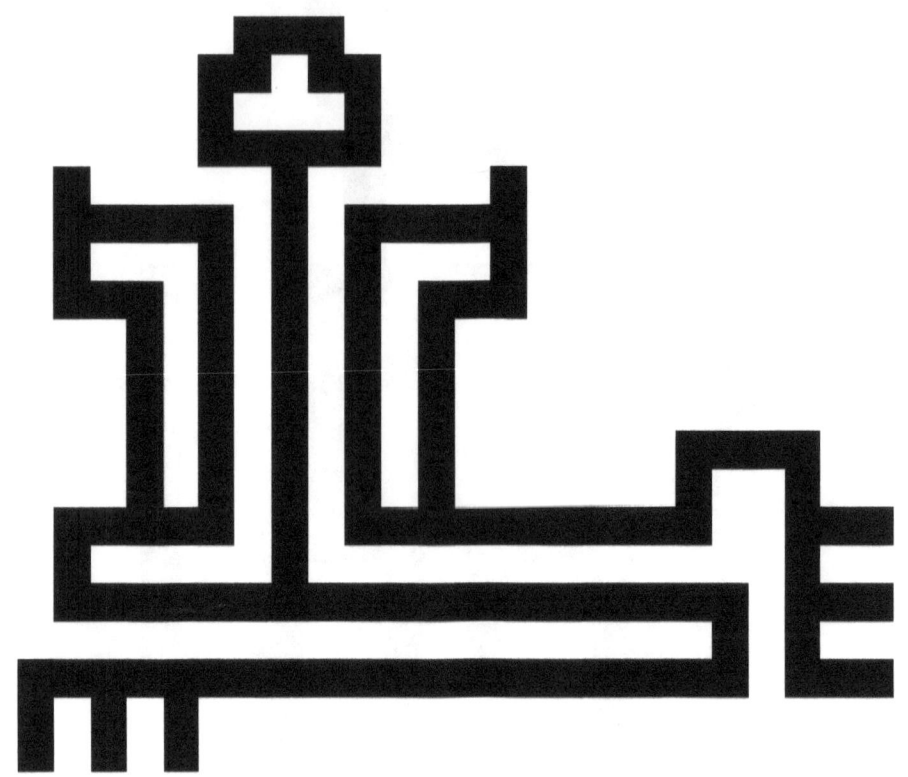

zohe zero

48

Xerox Sutra Editions is the grandmother
imprint of Xexoxial Editions. Expect
occasional publications in whims of
futuristic nostalgia. The first publications
of Xerox Sutra date September 1980
from Madison, Wisconsin. The name
was discontinued in 1985 when we
were threatened by a lawsuit from Xerox
Corporation for competing business
interests.

The font used in LOGOKONS is Glitch
Millennium, a 2003 remake of the original
Glitch font created by mIEKAL aND in
1987.

It can be downloaded for use from
www.xexoxial.org

www.ingramcontent.com/pod-product-compliance
Lightning Source LLC
Chambersburg PA
CBHW021921170526
45157CB00005B/2133